We expressly point out that external links contained in the text could only be viewed up to the time of the book's publication. The authors have no influence on later changes.

Concept by Team Zeitgeber

Marian Stoschitzky (Texts)
Klara Fleisch (Design)
Simon Bellink (Editing)
Saeed Helali

Special heartfelt thanks to

Center for Environmental Therapeutics
Dr. Michael Terman, President
Jessica Rao, Executive Director

Prof. Jamie Zeitzer,
Co-Director, Center for Sleep and Circadian Sciences,
Stanford University

First Edition
November 2023, Vienna

To all the night owls who want
to harness the light of day.

Content

Introduction

Mornings can feel terrible. If you know the pain of forcing your body out of bed against its desperate plea to stay there for longer, I feel you. Throughout my life, waking up had been a daily struggle. I was the guy to test tricks or available gadgets for better mornings - without much success. While it could have been seen as a mere inconvenience, this way of starting the day took a toll on my mindset and self-perception:

> *"How can I ever be in control of my life if I cannot even make it out of bed?"*

For me, it was days spent in nature when, literally, it dawned on me how things could be different. What if you could rise with the sun and feel good about it? What if you had the time to read, write or do sports before work? What if you could start the day at your self-determined pace? You can only know what quality time mornings can really be once you have experienced it. My experience in nature sparked my passion for the science behind enjoyable mornings. Today, I am part of the startup "*Zeitgeber*", with which we aim to make this fascinating science more available to the public. This course is our attempt to pass on what we have learned throughout the last years in the most concise form possible.

"*You're simply a night owl"* is what you may hear from other people or even tell yourself. Knowing what I know today, I regard this perspective as an unhealthy over-simplification of the matter. Do not get me wrong: It is a fact that people have different genetic dispositions regarding how their sleep-wake-timing is formed. Extreme forms, like "*delayed sleep phase disorder*" (DSPD) or other sleep-wake rhythm disorders can cause substantial suffering among affected people, with great difficulty following a rhythm that is normative despite their best efforts. Society is well-advised to acknowledge these inter-personal differences in "chrono-type" (genetic clock type) and to design corporate or school schedules accordingly. Despite all that, however, I want to make a case for two points:

- There is a lot you can do to influence when and how you wake up, probably more than you have thought. This book teaches you what you can do and why it works.

- Your current “natural” timing may not be as natural as you think. It may not be your healthiest setting, either.

To understand this, it is important to distinguish genetic disposition from actual timing: When you exclude pathological conditions, your sleep-wake cycle is always a result of your environment and lifestyle. Your genes will determine how your inner clock responds to certain environments and lifestyles: Differently for different people! At the end of the day, though, control over your environment and lifestyle, plus knowledge, means control over your biological clock. This knowledge is currently in your hands.

Unfortunately for you, the culture and environment in our Western world are far more geared towards *eveningness* than towards *morningness* (while ironically, morningness is often professionally required). For example, social activities or public events are usually set in the evening. This can make the maintenance of an early rhythm difficult and may have caused you to find yourself where you are. However, with the information provided in this book, you get the toolset to navigate your life in a way that is best for you.

The measures that enable you to rise earlier and with more energy are also measures that promote physical and mental health. Certain measures are even so beneficial that they are a recognized treatment for some forms of depression. They also promote better sleep and recovery as well as improved cognition and performance throughout the day. In a study from 2020[1], students implemented measures to achieve an earlier sleep-wake-cycle. Not only did they succeed in advancing it (by 2 hours on average), but they found themselves feeling better, sleeping better and performing better.

Your journey towards loving mornings really is one towards the healthiest and best version of yourself.

Having experienced these benefits ourselves, my colleagues from team Zeitgeber and I have made it our mission to support other people on their journey towards "circadian health" (the health of your daily biorhythm). We have distilled our knowledge from lots of scientific research, talks with international researchers as well as our own and other people's practical experiences into this book. It aims to provide you with the scientific understanding and science-based interventions to become more of a morning person and enjoy mornings for what they can be. Moreover, it will shed light on the factors that help or hinder a long-term implementation of a "*love mornings lifestyle*". In addition to the scientific part, you will find step-by-step practical guidance to follow over seven days. This inherent course helps you put your knowledge into practice.

If you have found yourself to get out of bed with difficulty, the transition to rising earlier will not come without effort in one or the other way. This is not your fault and you will learn to understand why that is. For the seven days of the course, though, I invite you to embrace this effort. Our goal is to let you know and experience what is possible so that you will be able to make an informed decision about what is best for you in the long run.

I invite you to follow the course with diligence. Have a glance at what is possible for you.

All the best,
Marian

What this book is not

- This book is not a magic pill to turn anyone into a morning person overnight. Change takes time and effort. There may be conditions under which the advice in the book may not be fruitful. This advice cannot substitute for a doctor's consultation if health issues impair your life.
- This book is not an anecdotal story of how *my* life got so much better, so *yours* will, too. It's not a description of "this one simple trick" that alone will make your life amazing.

What this book is

- This book is a science-based approach to an earlier, healthy sleep-wake cycle and better morning energy. It will give you the necessary scientific and practical understanding of how you can achieve it.
- In our guidance we will rely on best practices for habit-building to allow you to adopt desired actions. *Love mornings* is a holistic approach to behavioral and environmental changes, including routines, sleep hygiene, exercise, light exposure, nutrition, and more.
- This book aims to lay the foundation for a paradigm shift, making you see why and how the early bird's life can be something worth maintaining.

How to use this book

- You can read this book as a source of knowledge if you are curious about the science. If you want to read through it all at once - go ahead. However, this book is also designed as a course. If you aim to get results, do this: Select a week where you are in control of your sleep and wake time and free to choose your activity right before bedtime and right after waking up. Read one chapter every day.
- At the end of this book, you find a checklist we have made for you to use on a daily basis. Tick off the points you managed to comply with and track your results. Your list will start empty on Day 1. Throughout the course, you will fill in items when told to do so. If you prefer to print your checklist or use a digital format, find a 🔗 link to further tracking options at the end of chapter 1.
- If you encounter a yellow text box, you need to get active. Complete the action, then tick the checkbox to mark it as done. Some boxes depict "dailies" which are not to be ticked off right away but transferred into your checklist for daily execution.

☐ **To Do: Checklist**

Get familiar with the course checklist in the back of this book.

- If you anticipate difficulty staying consistent with your rhythm on a certain day (maybe you have a party to attend?), read the extra chapter "Cheat Days" at the back of the book.
- For all studies, books or quotes mentioned in the text, find the references in the chapter "Notes and Resources". Moreover, the chapter lists our recommended publications if you want to dive deeper into topics of the book.
- If you see this symbol 🔗 in the text you will find a QR link to further resources at the end of the chapter.

That is it! Let us get started – have you looked at the checklist? If so, it is time to tick off your first to-do.

Note: If you have a partner or live with other people, their attitudes towards your efforts matter: Tell them what you are up to or even get them on board to do this course with you. From experience, this will make your journey more enjoyable and increase your odds of success.

Resources Introduction: Scan to follow the 🔗 links

All your tracking options for this course (incl. checklist): *www.love-mornings.com/coursematerials#intro*

Day 1: Do no harm

Welcome to *love mornings!* In the upcoming two days, you will gain relevant knowledge on sleep and the circadian rhythm, which is your body's biological clock.

To start, let us get familiar with the factors that regulate your sleep: What makes you alert and what makes you sleepy? I want to introduce three factors which can greatly influence how you will feel in the morning:

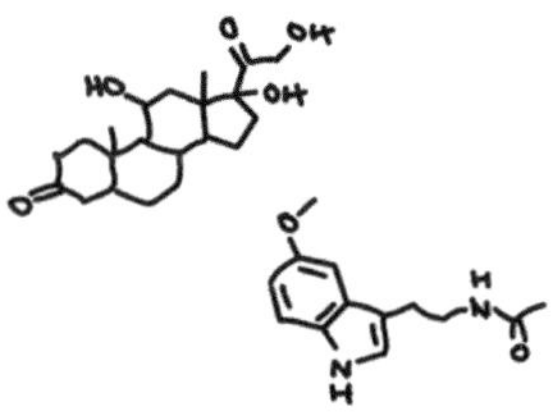

1. **Melatonin and cortisol** are the "tiredness" and "alertness" hormones

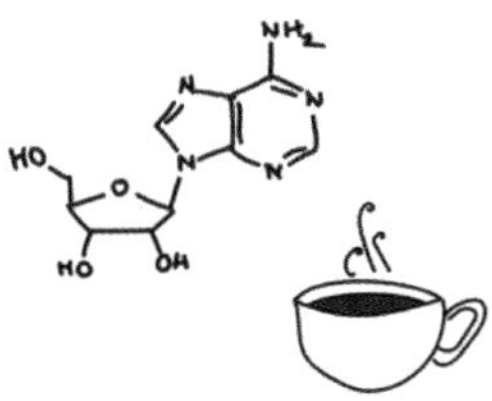

2. **Adenosine** is a neuro-transmitter responsible for your so-called "sleep pressure"

3. **Sleep hygiene** is important for the overall quality and quantity of your sleep

Sleep is naturally regulated by factors one and two. Sleep hygiene, the third point, has a significant influence not only on the timing of your sleep but also on how well you let points one and two do their natural jobs. But there is a catch: It is much easier to do harm than good. All the positive influences you will learn about will get heavily compromised if you do not keep your lifestyle clean from negative influences. You will notice that abstaining from hindering factors alone can make a huge difference in how you get out of bed, sleep, and your overall quality of life. Let us look at these factors in more detail:

Melatonin and cortisol

Your level of alertness throughout the day is regulated by hormones: Cortisol (which you may know as the *stress hormone*) is dominant throughout the day and fades out towards the evening. Melatonin, the *sleep hormone*, is released in the evening and overnight. It makes you tired and prepared for a good night's rest with all its restorative, anti-aging processes. The release of melatonin starts, on average, about two hours before your habitual bedtime. So far, so good.

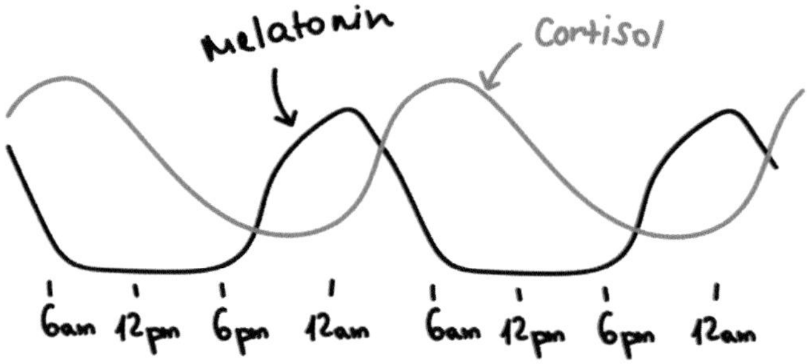

Melatonin makes you tired in the evening. But: Melatonin can be potently suppressed by light. And that is what almost all of us do every evening: They suppress their melatonin by using artificial lighting or looking at screens.

How light affects tiredness

Your eye has, besides the rods and cones for vision, some sort of "daylight sensor" cells in the retina (*intrinsically photo-sensitive retinal ganglion cells*). These cells report the level of illuminance to your brain, which controls the release of melatonin. The brighter the light, the more your brain thinks it is day. Also, the more blue is in the spectral composition of the light, the more your brain thinks it is day. Evolutionarily, this makes a lot of sense. Once the sun had set, the only light sources were moonlight, starlight or fire. Those are really dim and have little to no blue in their spectrum. If there was bright white light, it meant that either it was day or your place was on fire, and these are both good reasons to be alert.

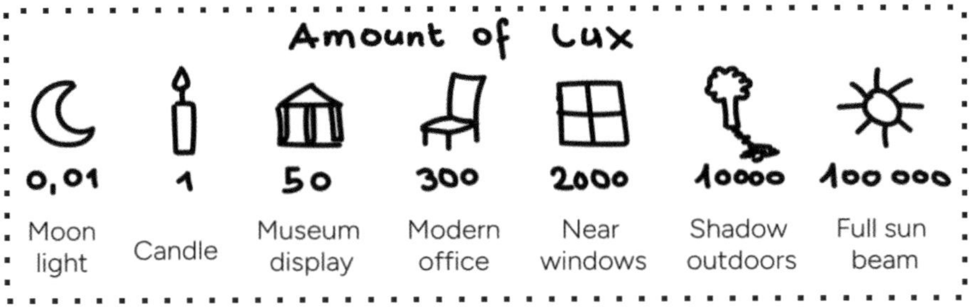

As a result of this, even low amounts of light at nighttime can have a significant impact on your melatonin levels. And that is a huge trap: You enjoy your evening plans and think you are not tired while you would be if it was dark. Your body just does not have the chance to tell you.

An international consortium of researchers recommends keeping light intensity below 1 lux at night[2]. That is the light intensity you get from a candle at a 1 m (or 3 ft) distance. It is barely enough to read a book! For the evening, it is 10 lux, which is still very little. However, anything above that has been shown to suppress melatonin in some people. Light sources, such as smartphone screens or light bulbs, easily go way beyond this threshold. It is worth noting that some people are more, some less sensitive to light. If you struggle to get out of bed in the morning, chances are you are part of the more sensitive group. Hence, what you want to do is avoid artificial light at night as much as you can.

Day	> 250 lux
Evening	< 10 lux
Night	< 1 lux

Recommendations for your light environment

Note: Dare to use candles as the number one solution, as they are dim, atmospheric and have basically no blue light in their spectrum. Set them up in well-ventilated places or use beeswax candles to avoid air pollution. For more information follow the 🔗 at the end of the chapter.

If you are interested in working with smart light bulbs, there are suppliers and programs with which you can automatically set healthy levels of brightness and color spectrum. Find 🔗 recommendations and more at the end of the chapter.

To Do: Light intensity

Download an app to measure light intensity (lux) in your environment. Go and compare some lux intensities of your home in the evening - where is little light, where might it be too much? Find the 🔗 links to the apps we use to measure light intensity at the end of the chapter.

Daily: Dim lights

Set the time to dim the lights to 2 hours before your desired bedtime. Write the time in your checklist (light bulb symbol) and stick to it for the rest of the course.

To Do: Evening Light Ambience

Eliminate all blue-ish light sources from your evening ambience. Reduce the ambient light to as little lux as possible (just enough to see your surroundings). If you use smart light bulbs that are dimmable or even dynamic in spectrum, make use of that feature. Keep in mind that your eyes can adapt to different intensities, so give your eyes about 5 minutes to adjust before making a judgment.

There are special glasses on the market called "blue light blockers" that filter out most of the blue parts of the light. Those can be useful in some cases, especially when you have limited control over your light environment. Note, however, that they mainly focus on the light spectrum and not on intensity and that the filtering is usually not perfect. As a rule of thumb, focus on light intensity as your most important factor. Therefore, while supportive, blue light blockers will not be a substitute for an optimized evening light environment. Among blue light blockers, only those with a clearly yellow or orange tint can actually help. Find recommendations and more on them in our tools section on our 🔗 website.

Your electronic devices are incredibly potent in stopping you from sleeping or sleeping well. The lighting is an easy win you can get here. You can digitally put an orange tint on your digital screens using freely available software, find the 🔗 links at the end of the chapter.

Bear in mind, however, that digital filters are also far from perfect. Abstaining from screen exposure at night is the best way to deal with it.

To Do: No blue screen light

Use a scheduled blue-light filter for your screens. If available, make sure adaptive dimming is on. For your smartphone, both iOS and Android support it out of the box. For your computer monitor, Windows and MacOS also support it.

Sleep Pressure: Adenosine

The longer you are awake, the more you feel the urge to sleep. That's intuitive, and you may have experienced the immense level of sleepiness yourself after, say, an all-nighter. When you have accumulated enough sleep pressure, you can virtually lie down anywhere and fall asleep. The key regulating factor behind this process is adenosine, a neuro-transmitter. This molecule binds to specific neuro-receptors in your brain, which manage various processes, including sleep pressure. The longer you are awake, the more adenosine will be bound to the responsible neuro-receptors, until you finally sleep. During sleep, adenosine is removed from the receptors, which resets your level of sleep pressure. By getting enough sleep, your body can reset the sleep pressure to zero and be fully awake again.

The crux of caffeine

Like with melatonin and cortisol, sleep pressure is naturally regulated by your body, but there is one particular external influence that potently tampers with it: caffeine. Caffeine binds to the same receptors as adenosine but does not make you tired. If caffeine blocks your adenosine receptors, the adenosine itself does not have the chance to get there and thus, you will not experience the sleep pressure caused by it. This intriguing mechanism is not exclusive to coffee: The active compound can be found in other drinks such as tea, cola, energy drinks and even in chocolate.

Now, here is the downside: You *need* sleep pressure to fall asleep. If your adenosine receptors are blocked, you may be tired (due to melatonin) but have severe trouble falling asleep. You are tired but not sleepy. A racing mind and the feeling of alertness that can feel incredibly troublesome in bed often have their roots in a lack of sleep pressure due to caffeine. And even if you do fall asleep, that sleep is likely not as restorative as it could be. Do not fret, you can still have your coffee and still become a morning person, but there might be some adjustments you need to follow through with.

Caffeine in your body has an average half-life of four hours. This means half of it will have been metabolized after this time, and half will remain. If you consume a coffee with 100 mg of caffeine, then after four hours, you will still have around 50 mg of caffeine in your body. This corresponds to more than a can of coke. After eight hours, there will still be 25 mg, which is still quite a bit! You get the idea: Getting rid of caffeine takes time! This is why a recent literature review[3] recommends to consume coffee no later than 8.8 hours before bedtime (4 p.m. for a bedtime at 10:48 pm), and people who take sleep very importantly would advise you not to consume it after 2 p.m. or even noon[4,5]. Decide for yourself which deadline to follow but do set a specific time. Being explicit about it will help you be consistent. The benefits of permitting sleep pressure in the evening are the key to successfully sleeping, which can then translate into more energetic mornings.

Daily: Caffeine deadline

Set a daily personal deadline for caffeine intake and stick to it. Make it 4 p.m. at the latest and earlier if you sometimes have trouble falling asleep at night. Write your deadline in the checklist (coffee symbol).

Sleep hygiene: Relaxation

Why are smartphones so bad for good sleep? Light is only one part of the equation. The other one is stimulation. Social Media, Youtube, TV, Netflix, etc. - content that is typically consumed over the internet is designed to cause arousal. This can be detrimental to a good night's sleep. Even under very dim lighting conditions, engaging smartphone content in the evening can delay sleep onset and lower sleep quality, as a study has shown[6]. Moreover, digital media are made to not only capture but keep your attention. *"Our biggest competitor is sleep"* is what Reed Hastings, founder of Netflix, stated in 2017[7]. As will be discussed in Chapter 6 in more detail, digital devices can make it very challenging to go to sleep at your desired bedtime. This is problematic since, as you may have guessed, getting enough sleep is a major factor in how refreshed you will feel the next day. The inconvenient truth is: Avoiding digital devices before bedtime may be one of the most beneficial things to do for your sleep. This can feel really hard, but it is also one of the biggest levers towards quality mornings.

Establishing a no-screen policy for the night has had a substantial positive effect on my life, literally overnight. I highly encourage you to try it if you do not already do so.

You will notice how you will gain an hour to spend with other pleasant things: Reading a book, journalling, spending time with a loved one, or just going to bed earlier. Disconnecting from the web at night paves the way for a healthy, self-determined life.

To Do: Screentime

Do not use digital devices or anything that connects to the internet for at least 1 hour before your habitual bedtime. Write your deadline in the checklist (phone symbol).

Note: Even with the right intentions, abstaining from digital media at night can be a really challenging task. Consider this not your lack of willpower, it is how these products were designed to work. Dare to make use of apps that help you with screen time restrictions - they have helped us a lot. Find our 🔗 recommendations at the end of the chapter.

Morning preparation

Having completed the to-dos so far, you should be rewarded with a relaxed evening. But let us not forget about our main goal: Loving mornings! For tomorrow, you will tackle this quite directly: What would make tomorrow morning something to love? What is something you would like to wake up for?

For me, this would be a 20-minute morning jog while listening to a preselected podcast episode. I would download the episode and then prepare my running gear, phone and headphones to readily wait for me the next morning. You may instead read a book (this book 😊), enjoy a good breakfast or watch the next episode of your favorite Netflix show. You should feel good in anticipation of your morning. Whatever it is, think it through timewise, write your plan on paper and prepare for it in a way that starting it will not cost you any cognitive effort the next day.

To Do: Reward

Define something enjoyable to wake up for tomorrow morning.

Daily: Preparation

Prepare everything necessary so you can start doing your rewarding thing in the early morning hours. Write "morning preparation" into the checklist (alarm clock symbol).

As a last to-do, schedule a time to continue with Day 2 of this book. Write it into your calendar. Scheduling is a great way to make you stick to something.

A great morning awaits you tomorrow, so make sure you get up at your desired time. Hard enough! But do wake up at the set time. I believe in you! You will be proud once you have done it.

See you tomorrow!

To Do: Block time

Block a time for reading Chapter 2 of this course.

Summary Chapter 1: Remember this

- Two separate factors mainly contribute to your evening tiredness: The hormone melatonin causes tiredness based on time of day. The neuro-transmitter adenosine causes more sleep pressure based on the duration you are awake until then.
- Melatonin can be potently suppressed by light. If you want to feel tired, dim the lights at night.
- Sleep pressure can be potently suppressed by caffeine. If you want to be able to fall asleep and sleep well throughout the night, do not consume caffeine in the second half of the day.
- Digital media can compromise your sleep not only due to the light from screens, but also due to the arousal and maintained engagement caused by its content.
- Start your *love mornings* journey by abstaining from hinderances. Instead, plan and prepare for a morning activity that you look forward to.

Resources Chapter 1: Scan to follow the 🔗 links

All your tracking options for this course (incl. checklist):
www.love-mornings.com/coursematerials#day1

Apps to measure light intensity for Android and iOS:
www.love-mornings.com/tools/lightmeter

Recommendations and more information on
beeswax candles, smart light, blue light blocking glasses & more:
www.love-mornings.com/tools

Software to help reduce screen time:
www.love-mornings.com/tools/screentimesoftware

Day 2: Circadian rhythm

Welcome back! I hope you got to enjoy a good morning! Have you filled in the checklist for yesterday evening and this morning? If so, awesome! If not, now is your chance to do so. Please rate your wake-up experience as well. If getting up was still tough, do not worry! That is what the next days are here for.

We have previously explored how direct measures such as abstaining from caffeine later in the day affect sleep and morning alertness. But how does your body know when to get tired (release melatonin) or to become intrinsically alert in the first place? Why do "night owls", tend to sleep in while others seem to just jump right out of bed? The answer to these questions lies in the fascinating field of chronobiology, the biology of your internal clock. Chronobiology holds the key to how you or anyone can truly become a morning person.

Chronobiology

Your body has multiple intrinsic senses of time. You may, for example, have heard about sleep cycles, which take 90 to 120 minutes and lead through varying brain activity during your sleep. Another type of cycle, which lasts around 28 days, is the menstrual cycle. What interests us in this book is the circadian rhythm: It is your internal clock cycle that stretches over roughly 24 hours. Its name *circadian* stems from Latin, combining "circa" (roughly) and "dies" (day).

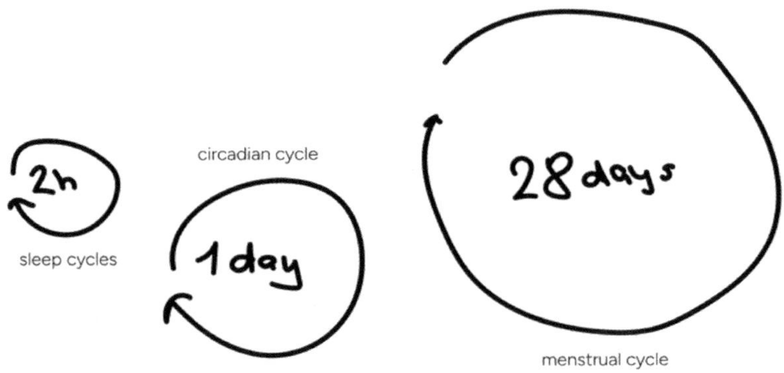

Technically, every cell in your body has its own circadian clock. However, your cells' clocks tend to align with the rhythm of the *supra-chiasmatic nucleus* (SCN) – a sort of "master clock" located in the hypothalamus in your brain. Therefore, "your circadian rhythm" as a singular term is a useful simplification that refers to the rhythm of your SCN master clock.

Circadian rhythms govern your natural sleep-wake-rhythm, digestion, peak performance timing, peak focus timing and more. Your circadian rhythm is an intrinsic phenomenon: This means that even in complete isolation from external influences, this daily rhythm keeps cycling. To prove this, researchers locked themselves in a cave under the earth for several weeks[8]. Indeed, their internal clock continued to tick.

While the illustration below depicts clock times as an estimate for the average circadian rhythm, there is quite some variation in biological timing

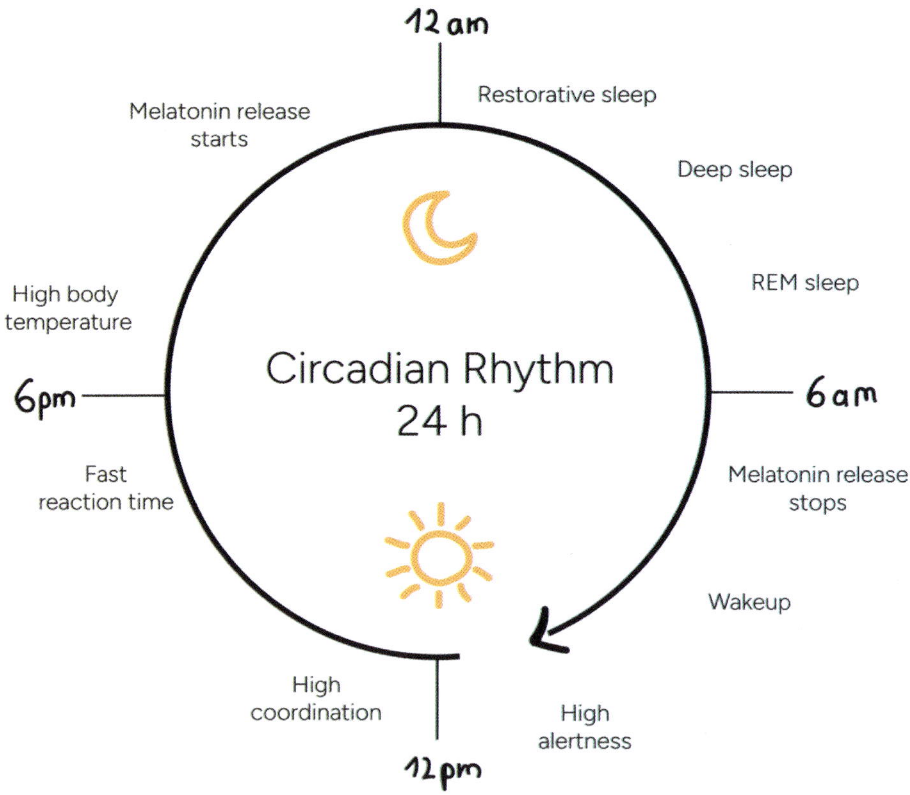

between people. In Western society, the median sleep schedule on free days is from midnight to 8 a.m., but there are larks (the early risers) who may naturally sleep from 9 p.m. to 5 a.m. and night owls who may naturally sleep from 4 a.m. to 12 p.m[9]. The biological preference for earlier or later schedules is referred to as "*chronotype*" (from the Greek "chronos" meaning "time"), with larks being "morning types" and night owls being "evening types".

Night owl
Tends to go to sleep and wake up late

Lark
Tends to go to sleep and wake up early

Circadian clock versus alarm clock

Let us for now focus on sleep-wake timing. In the last chapter, we have discussed that your body starts releasing the "tiredness hormone" melatonin in the evening. This starts about two hours before your natural bedtime. In the early morning, melatonin fades and your "alertness hormone" cortisol takes over, usually starting to rise a little bit before your natural wake time. Cortisol helps your body mobilize energy resources and makes it easier to get out of bed.

Now, what happens if you force yourself out of sleep prior to your natural wake time by using, for example, an alarm clock? Biologically, your body will still be in night-time mode, with significant amounts of melatonin and little cortisol. You will feel like your body would want you to feel at this point: tired!

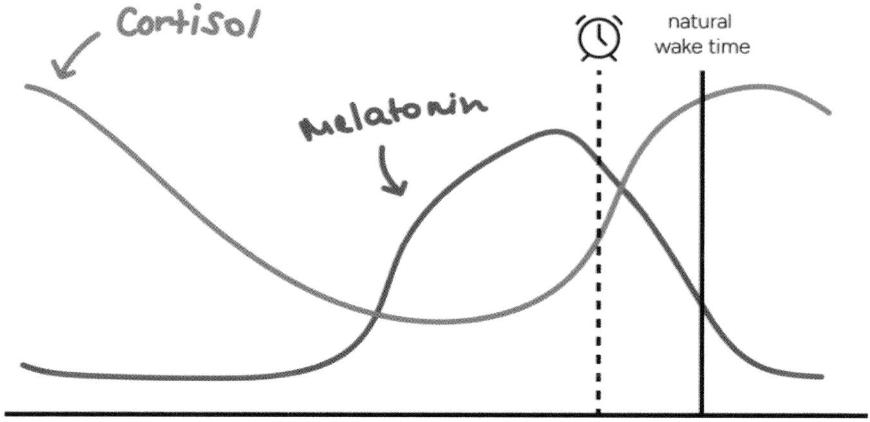

A large German survey[10] has shown that 7 out of 10 people wake up like this! During weekdays, 7 out of 10 people get up at least 1 hour before their natural wake-up time. No wonder people are tired in the morning! It is a similar game in the evenings: If you rationally know it would be a good time to go to bed, but for your circadian rhythm, it is not time yet, then you will not have a lot of melatonin in your blood. You will just not feel very tired and struggle to fall asleep. This is the exact phenomenon you experience when you have jet lag after traveling through time zones. Indeed, the phenomenon of rising unnaturally early during weekdays has been labeled "social jet lag" for its similarity to time zone travel[9].

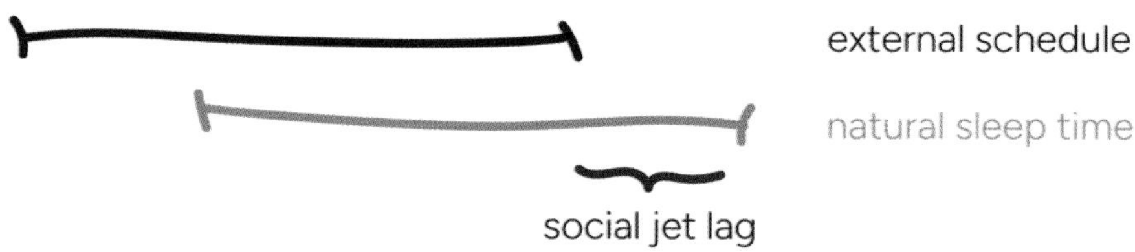

Early working hours make evening types particularly prone to this sort of misalignment. Both forced awakening and sleep debt (caused by a lack of evening tiredness) increase your morning tiredness. However, the adverse effects do not seem to stop there: While the exact causes are partly unclear, evening types face a higher long-term risk for... well, basically every lifestyle disease[11]: cardiovascular disease[12], obesity[13], diabetes[14], you name it. It is not a health risk as severe as smoking, but it is significant. Moreover, the evening chronotype is associated with a higher risk for depression[15]. Intense shift work, a systematic disruption of your circadian rhythm, has even been labeled "probably carcinogenic" (causing cancer) by the American Association for the Research on Cancer in 2019[16]. Living against your circadian clock is not healthy, and your morning tiredness is a kind reminder to work with your body and not against it.

How to shift your circadian rhythm

What can you do about it? To answer this question, you need to understand what determines your rhythm in the first place. As we have established, chronotypes in Western society span a broad spectrum of settings. How come that people's internal clocks run so different from one another? One influential factor is your genetic disposition, which makes people prone to being a lark or an owl. But being earlier or later always needs a reference, as biology has no absolute time. So, what is the reference your body synchronizes to? It is, you may have guessed it, light. Okay, let us be a little more precise: There are multiple stimuli that your body clock synchronizes to. These stimuli are scientifically called "*zeitgebers*", derived from the German "giving time". Zeitgebers include exercise, meal intake or sleep, which can all give a sense of whether it is day or night. However, light is the dominant zeitgeber and, if available, your body tends to prioritize light over other stimuli as far as your sleep-wake rhythm is concerned. This makes sense from an evolutionary standpoint since

- daylight has since the beginning of life served as the defining factor for night and day.
- it makes sense to be awake and alert during daylight hours, as you are more easily found and eaten by predators or enemies.

So, your circadian clock synchronizes to light (and other factors). How exactly does that happen? Your brain mainly uses two sensitive windows of the day to synchronize with the lighting schedule: Early morning and late night. If your retina senses sustained bright or increasing light in the morning, your brain assumes that the day has already started, and your circadian clock shifts towards an earlier schedule. The opposite is true for the late evening, where a lot of light pushes you towards eveningness. To what extent can you shift your circadian clock in one day? A study from Stanford University shows that the maximum lies around two hours for one day, at least in laboratory settings[17]. In real life, around 30 minutes are more realistic and already pretty good if you implement the proper measures.

Does all of this mean that, theoretically, you could shift your circadian rhythm to four hours earlier over a couple of days, just by changing your lighting schedule? 100%. You may have actually done that many times in your life already: It is precisely what happens when you travel towards the East, into a time zone four hours ahead of yours. By adapting to the light-dark cycle of this time zone, relative to your original rhythm, you will rise and sleep four hours earlier than usual, becoming a super early riser. The problem is, so does your entire environment, including the external clock time. Therefore, relative to your local clock, you, originally a night owl, will again find yourself as a night owl there.

What if you turn this experiment around and enforce eveningness? You do not have to travel for this: What if you get up early regularly, but it is still dark outside, and you do not get sufficient bright light in the morning? Despite pursuing an early-morning lifestyle, you may maintain your late rhythm because your circadian clock lacks the necessary stimuli to adjust accordingly. To make matters worse, if you then spend your evenings under a lot of artificial light, be it your room light or digital screens in front of you, you may even shift towards a *later* circadian rhythm despite rising *early* every day. Your social jet lag increases, and so do your difficulties getting out of bed.

This is exactly what is happening in our society, and it is a huge problem! Remember that circadian misalignment is linked to worse health, physically and mentally, besides the apparent struggle out of bed? How we handle our light exposure is absurd when considering societal health and well-being. Contributing to the improvement of this situation is the main driver behind this book. You can only act on it as an individual if you know about the implications of your (lighting) actions on your biology. Well, now you know. 🙄

So, on towards ways to improve your situation.

Getting rid of social jet lag

Let us look again at light exposure in nature: In the morning, the dawn announces the day. Then, there is bright daylight throughout the day until the sun sets. Afterwards, there is practically no biologically relevant light, since your circadian system, just like melatonin, is most sensitive to bright or blue light. Nature provided people in pre-industrial times with a stable lighting schedule, changing only slowly with the seasons. Consequently, such lighting conditions led to a very steady circadian rhythm for humans. Those were the days...!

Nowadays, most people sleep in darkness until they rise due to an alarm clock. They also spend 90% of their time indoors, under lighting conditions that, for your brain, are somewhere in the twilight range and not full-day-bright. This artificial light persists, however, until late into the evening, until people go to bed. What a confusion for your circadian clock! If you were that clock, what would you do? Since all it can really tell is that at night-time, there is still light, it is quite understandable that your clock tends to shift towards night-time every day. You notice it by being less tired in the evening and more tired in the morning, which reinforces late-night activity.

Would that mean that, by re-gaining a "naturalistic" lighting schedule, people who are night owls could switch back to a more average circadian rhythm? University professor Kenneth Wright in Colorado investigated this exact hypothesis[18]. He selected students who considered themselves night owls and took measurements to assess their circadian phase, i.e. their internal clock time. Then, he sent the students camping for a week without any artificial light. For this week, they lived under the light conditions our ancestors once had.

Assessing their circadian phase again after that week, Wright found that the students had indeed adopted an earlier rhythm. The difference was 2 hours on average and was greater the later their rhythm had initially been (one of the students shifted over 4.5 hours!)[18]. Wright and his team later conducted a similar study to find that 69% of the shift is produced by just a weekend of camping[19]. Light really is a potent agent here.

What actions can you take to benefit from this advice in practice?

Evening

I can only repeat the importance of dimming your lights at night (see Day 1). Now, you know that evening light leads not only to the acute suppression of tiredness but also to a delayed circadian rhythm. If you want to transition towards morningness, you do want to avoid that!

Morning preparation

Before you can start adjusting your rhythm, you need to define where you want to go. What should become your natural sleep-wake rhythm? This is an essential question because your goal will be to stick to the same schedule throughout this course. You can challenge yourself with an early schedule to see what is possible if that is what you want. However, I encourage you to find a rhythm that you consider appealing in the long term and would like to establish for your life. This is particularly important regarding your bedtime, where a very early schedule may conflict with your social life. Mind your body's need for sleep: Plan in a way that allows for a sleep duration which feels good for you (for most people, this lies between 7-9 hours per night). Don't try to minimize the time in bed; rather, try to establish a healthy routine.

To Do: Time commitment

Define at which time you commit to wake up and a "bedtime" at which you want to be ready for sleep (that can mean being in bed, but also reading or meditating. Do not force yourself to try to fall asleep if you are not tired). Make sure the times add up to the amount of sleep you need plus, preferably, > 15 min extra buffer. Write the times in the checklist.

Congratulations on that step! Now, consider leveraging social accountability to strengthen your commitment. This may seem weird, but it is a powerful tool in behavioral psychology. Sharing your commitment with another person can help you stay consistent in difficult moments and get where you want to go.

To Do: Social commitment

Commit, in written form, to a person of choice that you are going to get up at your defined time for the rest of this course. You can as well add a financial incentive to it, too. "For every morning risen later than ___ a.m., I will give you $ 10." Stick to your commitment.

Optional To Do: Public announcement

If you want to be bold, publish your commitment on social media (for example our reddit channel r/lovemornings).

All set? Great! Now, let us take action to reset your circadian rhythm. Morning bright light exposure is the key activity to get you there. Already, brief durations of 10–30 minutes have been shown to affect people's rhythm, providing the most considerable shift per minute of light exposure[20]. If you have the time, though, longer durations (up to 6.5 hours have been investigated) do amplify the effect. To maximize your results, feel free to extend your light exposure to one hour or more. If you have little flexibility in the morning, this is of course not an option. Feel free to get creative in finding 10+ minutes of morning bright light exposure! Maybe you could walk the first part of your way to work or school? Maybe you could have your coffee or tea on the balcony? Even if the sky is cloudy -

go outside, still. Use your light meter app to measure whether you get more than 1000 lux. If you do, you are fine.

Then again, there is winter. There may be days when you have to get up and leave the house before dawn. Naturally, this makes it impossible to get the necessary bright light exposure outdoors. How could you get to lux levels above 1000 lux indoors? You could assemble multiple desk lamps on your kitchen table to get your dose of bright light while having breakfast. Just make sure to not look directly into glaring light sources, to keep your eyes safe. If you currently lack the proper light equipment for this use case, a daylight lamp is the one thing out of all possible gadgets along the way that I would recommend the most - for better mornings, better mood and better health overall in winter, for that matter.

Find our recommended products for artificial morning bright light and dawn simulation in the tools section on our website.

Daily: Bright light

While or after waking up, expose yourself to bright light. If possible, go outside and view daylight for at least 10 minutes. The longer the better. The earlier the better. If there is no daylight available around your wake time, use a daylight lamp or your best available sources of bright artificial light. Write this in the checklist (sun symbol).

Optional To Do: Wake-up light

Use a wake-up light or smart light automation to have light accompany your wake-up process.

Studies have shown that waking up with wake-up lights makes it easier to get out of bed and can contribute to a better morning mood[21,22]. While the wake-up lights did not affect the circadian phase directly, they can facilitate the process overall.

Whatever duration or tools you choose, define them clearly and then try to stick to them. Remember to execute your daily tasks from yesterday's checklist, too, such as the preparation of your next morning. It might have changed a little now that you will expose yourself to bright light. If necessary, feel free to adapt your morning schedule, but make sure to have your latest plan written down and all the required items for the next day readily prepared before you go to bed.

24 hours?

The tricky part about your circadian rhythm is that your circadian clock is not set to precisely 24-hour cycles. In practice, it has been shown that its intrinsic cycle period is a little longer than that, on average 24:11 hours[23]. It is like a clock that is running a bit later every day. This means that when running idle, without external stimuli, you shift slightly towards eveningness. Evening types tend to have a more extended period length than early birds. Therefore, re-gaining a morning-friendly rhythm requires consistent action and morning light exposure. It is also worth noting that you need substantially less evening light to delay your clock than morning light to advance it. I am afraid convenience is not on your side. Yet, with the action plan that you are defining in this course, you are creating your best framework to get there.

One upside to finish with: Sleep researcher Charles Czeisler and his team at Harvard University have shown that when you expose yourself to bright light in the morning or throughout the day, your circadian sensitivity to evening light decreases, by up to 40%[24]. So, if you stick to your morning light routine, you help your rhythm become more resistant to evening light influences. Not only that, it also improves your mood to the extent that morning bright light is a recognized first-line treatment for winter depression[25]. It really does pay off!

See you tomorrow!

Summary Chapter 2: Remember this

- Your *circadian rhythm* is your body's internal clock which regulates your natural sleep-wake timing. It cycles roughly every 24 hours.
- Your *chronotype* describes how your circadian clock is timed relative to the local clock time. In Western society, there is a wide variety of chronotypes, ranging from very early risers to extreme night owls.
- A chronic misalignment between circadian clock and actual sleep-wake timing poses a risk to long-term health. Evening chronotypes are particularly prone to these health risks.
- You can shift your circadian clock time by exposing yourself to *zeitgeber* stimuli, notably light. Bright light exposure in the morning advances your clock while light in the evening delays it.
- To adopt an earlier circadian rhythm, avoid artificial light in the evening while making bright light exposure a part of your mornings. The more light you get in the morning, the more you will advance your circadian clock.

Resources Chapter 2: Scan to follow the 🔗 links

Recommendations and more information on
bright light/daylight lamps, light alarms, smart lights & more:
www.love-mornings.com/tools

Join our reddit community to discuss related topics, ask
questions or get to know like-minded people (us included):
www.reddit.com/r/lovemornings

Day 3: Routine

Congrats, Day 3 already! How was your enlightened morning? Please make sure to fill in the checklist. Amazing if you have managed to stick to your plans! 🙂

You may have already gotten some benefit out of your *love mornings* actions. If so, that is great! If getting up to view bright light was hard, do not worry. Be aware that the change process, whether in rhythm or behavior, is more energy-expensive than sustaining an established system. Things will get easier if you stay on track.

As we speak about it: staying on track is what today's chapter is about. To get the best results, it is vital to stick to what you want to do:

Effectiveness = Efficacy × Compliance

How effective this course is depends on how well its strategies work, but also how consistently you can implement them daily.

This chapter lays the foundation for behavioral patterns that will allow you to make the most out of this book, i.e. comply with the suggested tasks for the duration of the course and beyond. We will pick some cherries from behavioral psychology and neurophysiology to build routines, compliance mechanisms and ways to maintain motivation. Ideally, rising early will be rewarding and manageable, and you will have clarity about why you do what you do (or do not do).

Make rising early rewarding

It is in our nature to pursue actions based on the anticipated reward they bring (or the avoidance of pain, respectively). For some actions, the expected reward is clear and direct (I eat a cookie → I will like the taste). In other cases, we rely on our intelligence to connect a complex chain of actions with usually large, later-stage rewards (I will study for multiple hours a day for multiple years → I will have better professional opportunities and social status). However, as you may have experienced with social media while studying, or sweets on the table while on a diet, your brain is wired to crave quick rewards even if they may conflict with your longer-term goals. The allure of instant gratification is real and your cognitive battle against it requires energy. Acknowledging this, let us assess how satisfying rising early is for you: For many people, getting up at a certain time is a necessity (or desire) to get the work done that awaits them during the day. Ugh, you take upon yourself the effort of rising early just to do even more work during the day! Compare this to the instant, though short-lived relief of pressing the snooze button in the morning. Many people like the idea of rising early, but when it comes down to it, actually rising early is just not a pleasant experience for them.

How could you change that? It is much to ask from your dazed morning brain to connect the complex chain of actions to a later-stage reward. Instead, aim at improving the short-term rewards associated with rising early and staying in bed. You will get up if (and only if) the anticipated reward for getting up outweighs that of staying in bed. There are three ways to achieve this:

- Make getting up easier: You do this by getting enough high-quality sleep, shift your circadian clock and use wake-up lights or alarm clocks that make your wake-up experience more pleasant. We have already discussed this in Chapters 1 and 2.
- Increase the cost of staying in bed: You can achieve this by formulating a written contract with yourself, as done in Chapter 2, and leveraging social accountability to get up on time. If you have not yet promised to a friend that you will get up on time throughout the course, feel free to do so, now!
- Make getting up directly rewarding! This is where many people fall short. For your first morning, you have set yourself a pleasant task to enjoy. This is a good start! Let us now expand on this.

How can you associate waking up with something nice? Let us learn from Ivan Pawlow's dog experiments how to restructure your trigger-reward system in the morning more in your favor: Ivan Pawlow was a Russian physician and Nobel laureate, famous for his work on conditional reflexes[26]. By ringing a bell every time he provided food for his dogs, the dogs started to associate the sound of a bell with food. After some time, the sound of the bell, a stimulus which alone had nothing to do with food, was enough to trigger an increase in saliva in the dogs' mouths, which is a reflex in anticipation of food.

We can leverage conditional reflexes to connect getting up with an immediate reward: The idea behind this is taken from Sam Uyama's short but intriguing book "*How to Love Waking Up*"[27]. With the help of a daily honey-coated almond on his nightstand (among other things), the author managed to become a fully-fledged morning person. Having tested the "immediate reward" approach within our team, we, too, found it oddly beneficial. Something small (and maybe sweet) to eat can be a suitable reward. Feel free to get creative if you do not like to eat in the morning. Perhaps you prefer a calendar with a daily quote? Perhaps you want to see a new message from a loved one which you are only allowed view at wake time? Whatever it is, make sure you treat yourself directly after getting out of bed.

When considering the reward, a sense of surprise in the reward may make your compliance even better (inspired by Nir Eyal's book *"Hooked"*)[28]. Scientifically, this is called *random intermittent reward* structure. It means that you do not know how great your reward will be (but it could be something you really like!). Intermittent rewards have been found to be even more motivating (and even addicting) than fixed rewards. They are considered the driving force behind social media and gambling. Some more suggestions for wake-up rewards are:

- Listening to a song you like
- Listening to or reading the news
- Applying a nice face cream
- Smelling essential oils you like
- Cuddling with your partner (or dog 🐶)

☐ To Do: Reward

Find a reward to treat yourself with daily, immediately after getting out of bed (punctually) and turning off your alarm. It is important that the reward is readily available (e.g. waiting for you on your night stand), immediate and that you actually like it.

Let your reward be exclusive to this time of day: This means that if you choose applying a certain face cream as a reward, make it more special by not applying facial cream during other times of the day.

It may feel weird to condition yourself like this. Keep in mind, though, that most parts of your brain are quite primeval and appreciate incentivization the way dogs or other animals would. Even after you have successfully gotten out of bed, the more rewarding your first minutes of the day feel, the more likely you are to adopt rising early as a habit. Keep this in mind when designing your morning routine.

Your morning routine

How are you going to spend your mornings? Some actions, like viewing bright light, help you shift towards an earlier rhythm on a biological level. These actions are set for now. The rest of the morning is yours to decide. If you already have ideas, a routine will help you structure them. You will turn your intentions into an organized and realistic plan.

This plan is called a morning routine. I am happy to share mine with you. Every morning, I go through the following steps:

7:00 - Get up & eat sweet reward
7:00 - 7:05 - Get dressed and ready to go outside
7:05 - 7:25 - Outside exercise routine (while listening to a podcast)
7:25 - 7:35 - Shower & brush teeth
7:35 - 7:40 – Prepare breakfast
7:40 - 8:00 – Enjoy breakfast (feels like a reward as well)

My routine takes me 60 minutes every day. Only then, I look at my phone for all the messages and tasks that await me for the day. I try to keep the same routine every day, even on weekends. Being human, I sometimes struggle to comply with the exercise part. I motivate myself with music or, if too tired, skip it and fall back to getting bright light from a daylight lamp during breakfast. Having one "full" and one "core" version of your routine can be a help to keep some flexibility (find a case study later in the chapter for more inspiration on this).

Your morning activities can greatly impact your morning energy level and set your mindset for the day. Your options range from yoga over pursuing a personal project or reading to simply taking the time to enjoy a healthy breakfast. Last but not least, you can choose to do nothing additional at all if your work starts early and all you want is to get out of bed more easily.

Whatever else your routine encompasses, what I require you to do for the course is to expose yourself to bright light in the morning. Use the first minutes of your waking day for at least 10 minutes of daylight exposure if the sun is already out at this time of year. As you read yesterday, daylight is an enormous help on your journey. Ideally, go outside and do something active like jumping around, jogging, yoga/workout, or just walking. If that feels out of reach right now, start with 10+ minutes sitting on the balcony or next to an open window. If it is winter or the sun rises too late for your wake time, get your bright light from your best available artificial light source.

You will get your best results if you stay consistent in your wake time and the timing of light exposure throughout all days of the week. When you anticipate difficulties regarding that, feel free to write down alternatives for certain days days or for individual activites - maybe one day, you really do not feel like doing meditation but would instead read a book. That is fine! Just write down what the alternatives are.

To Do: Morning routine

Use the "routines" template in the back of the book to draft your morning routine. Plan the start of your day in time blocks of certain activities. Make your routine as long or short as feels comfortable to you.

A note of caution: While an exhaustive morning routine may appear intriguing to some, your routine should be one that you will realistically want to do for the next four days and even beyond. Do not exaggerate in what you expect from yourself. Most importantly:

Make your mornings something rewarding to look forward to.

EXAMPLE ROUTINE

MORNING

TIME	ACTIVITY
06:30	get up together, toilet, drink glass of water
06:35	reward for not hitting snooze: enjoy balcony
06:40	breathwork session OR meditation session
06:50	yoga stretching; OR intense quick workout
07:00	prepare + eat breakfast, listen to news
07:20	brush teeth, take a shower, get dressed
07:40	start the day / go to work

(06:35–07:00: outside)

EVENING

TIME	ACTIVITY
21:30	dim all the lights, last chance to check phone
	floss, brush teeth, put on pyjama
21:40	wind down breathing OR relax yoga
21:50	journal + prep next day
22:00	go to bed & enjoy undistracted time together
22:30	go to sleep

If you are still open for inspiration regarding your routine, here is a case study from *Simon*, who has been among the early users of this course. What Simon says about this routine:

> *"It took us about two weeks to fully adapt the routine to our needs. Doing it as a couple added great value for us, as we can motivate each other and enjoy the additional time spent together. We realized that giving ourselves some options to choose from in some blocks helps us staying consistent overall, as there is always an easier option to go for in case you just don't feel like working hard that day – which is then not a dealbreaker anymore. Keeping the rhythm is what matters most to us."*

One last thing I want to bring to your attention as a possible part of your morning routine: A gratitude journal. It involves writing down things you're grateful for each day. This helps you to focus on the positive aspects of your life and appreciate the good things, no matter how small they may be. A routine backed by science to improve mental well-being is the 5-minute journal, which includes gratitude, goals and affirmations in the morning. It has been part of my routine for years, and I still like it a lot. We even designed and released our 🔗 own version of the journal.

Lower the friction

Imagine you plan to lift weights in the morning. How often will you stay true to your commitment? I can confidently tell you that the answer will be "never" if you do not have any weights at home (and no gym nearby). It is critical for your success to make starting your behavior realistic and easy. Even if you do have weights at home, storing them in a box or under the bed can make staying consistent with your actions challenging.

> *"To initiate action, doing must be easier than thinking. Remember, a habit is a behavior done with little or no conscious thought. The more effort - either physical or mental - required to perform the desired action, the less likely it is to occur."*
> – Nir Eyal, author of "Hooked"[28]

To lift weights in the morning, you want your weights to already stand there waiting for you. Now, what does that mean for you and your routine? Of course, there are not only behaviors that you want to adopt, but also such that you habitually perform but want to get rid of: Distractions. Note that the advice on friction can work the other way as well: Increase the friction towards undesired behaviors!

To Do: Item preparation

Think about what clothes or items your morning routine requires. Write the items next to the activities in your routine 🔗 template, so that you have a written list of what to prepare for the next day before you go to bed.

Why are smartphones so alluring? They are a portal to instant gratification that can be opened at the push of a button. Opening your smartphone screen requires no cognitive effort whatsoever. You can perform it without conscious thought. Your brain will be rewarded with novel content and, thus, reinforced. However, you may lose a lot of time along the way, spending minutes to hours on your phone. To change this pattern, you can increase the friction towards checking your phone. Already a low barrier may lead to drastic results! After installing the app *"HelpMeFocus"* on my Android phone, my YouTube and Instagram consumption dropped from well over an hour a day to almost zero. All the app does is require you to type a randomly generated sequence of characters before you can access undesired apps. One prompt buys you two minutes of screen time. The ten seconds of cognitive effort required to open an app can be enough to think twice about whether you really want to go on that watching spree.

Keep friction in mind when you seem to repeatedly indulge in undesired behaviors. I invite you not to be hard on yourself for a lack of discipline, but smart at increasing or lowering friction wherever useful.

Note: Find suitable options for distraction blockers across all platforms in the tools section on our 🔗 website.

Your evening routine

Besides your morning routine, a clear, written-down evening routine is a powerful tool, too. Having your actions scheduled will help you be intentional about them and stop the perception of "not having anything better to do" in the evening, which would make you vulnerable to unhealthy distractions (of course, any activity is fair if deliberately chosen.) A clear plan may help you enjoy intentional me-time to wind down and relax. If you have a partner or a family, dare to be open about your routine. Invite them to draft evening routines for themselves or, as desired, even integrate them into your routine.

Within your evening routine, please block time to perform the following daily tasks:

- Prepare clothes for the next day's morning activity
- Prepare your reward for getting up
- Use your journal or some paper to write down a rough plan of the next day's most important elements

To Do: Evening routine

Like with your morning routine, draw your evening routine on the provided template and let it end with your scheduled bedtime.

This preparation will help you make your desired actions your reality for the next day, take mental load off your brain and increase your odds for compliance by having already invested in your desired actions. Moreover, a study has shown that planning the next day before going to bed can even help you fall asleep faster[29]. Therefore, try really writing things down instead of just thinking about them.

In case you, for any reason, do not comply with your evening routine in its entirety, do stick to the two tasks above as its core version before you go to bed, still. If you brush your teeth before bed, put this at equal importance.

Know your "why"

So far, this chapter has taught you how the right preparation can facilitate your desired actions. Designing your day and environment in a smart way is often more powerful than relying on mere willpower. Sometimes, though, willpower is still needed. There may be days when your sleep-wake-rhythm gets disrupted, or you just do not have a lot of energy. How can you come up with the motivation to still stick to your plans? This is where being clear about your "why" can be of invaluable help. Having a "why" means that you know the motivations that drive your actions.

Put yourself in the shoes of your just-woken-up self, one month from now: You may have gone to bed later than desired the previous night. You feel sleepy. You may be tempted to sleep just a little longer. I want to ask you:

Why would you still want to get up, despite all inconvenience?

There is a neurophysiological reason why having a "why" is important: Dopamine. Dopamine is a neurotransmitter and your brain's resource to bring up the mental energy to do tasks. Your brain's dopamine release can be triggered by various factors: It may be the anticipation of a reward but also an audience cheering for you, humor, or motivational music, among other things. All these factors can help you to push yourself and put in the mental effort required to do something. Notably, the feeling of being on the right track also triggers a dopamine release. If you have a "why" to get up in the morning, acting accordingly means you are making progress towards the goal that your "why" represents. This anticipation of progress results in a release of dopamine, which will greatly facilitate your action.

So, what is your reason to get up in the morning? Ideally, it is something that you feel strongly about, which stands above mere convenience, and which prioritizes getting up unquestionably higher than staying asleep.
If you are not clear about your "why" right away, start your reflection here: Why did you start reading this book in the first place? It may have to do with your life being self-determined? Maybe it relates to a personal or professional goal? Or do you want to have more time with your partner or family? Finding and clearly stating your why can be a daunting task. I invite you to consider your values, passions and goals for your life. What outlook

gets you excited? Which goal gives you a sense of fulfilment? Why would rising early be significantly better than alternative realities?

Some examples for whys we love:

- I want to get up to finish my graphics design course to switch careers
- If I get up at my set time and do my morning routine, I will feel better throughout the day
- I want to be an early riser to spend quality time with my partner to strengthen our relationship

If you struggle to find a clear "why" even after having given it significant thought, this is okay. Take your best candidate and, if needed, re-iterate after some time. It is okay even to decide against waking up early if you consider it the better option for you after finishing this book. Until then, consider this "why": To find out whether this book can help you, you need to value your commitment: You can only be a qualified judge of this course's effect on your life if you stick to it.

Congratulations, you have made it through Day 3! Remember that consistent action can feel challenging. With the to-dos from this chapter, you are prepared to make it through the course with the highest possible chance of success. Way to go!

To Do: Define a „why"

Define a „why" for yourself to keep diligently following this course's recommendations. Let your why be concise and effective enough to win against internal counterarguments of a sleepy early-morning mind. Write it down in the bottom of the checklist.

Optional To Do: Alarm text

If you use an alarm clock app that supports a custom alarm text, replace your current text with the "why" you have identified. This way, your alarm clock will directly remind me of your motivations when you get up.

Summary Chapter 3: Remember this

- You will get out of bed on time if and only if the anticipated reward of getting up is higher than that of staying in bed.
- You can increase the reward associated with getting up by coupling the action with a quick reward, such as a small sweet to eat right after getting out of bed.
- A morning routine helps you spend your mornings the way you want without actively thinking about your actions every day.
- By preparing everything you need for your morning routine in advance, you make it easier for yourself to stick to your plans.
- An evening routine can help you be intentional about your evening activities, find relaxation and facilitate a good morning the next day.
- When sticking to your plans feels difficult, knowing your "why" can help you overcome mental barriers.

Resources Chapter 3: Scan to follow the 🔗 links

Our own 5-min journal and other recommendations:
www.love-mornings.com/tools/journals

The printable version of your routine template:
www.love-mornings.com/coursematerials#day3

Software to help minimize distractions across all platforms:
www.love-mornings.com/tools/distraction

Day 4: Body temperature

Let us dive a little deeper into the science of circadian rhythm. You may know by now that our hormonal levels of cortisol and melatonin follow a circadian rhythm. But hormonal secretion is by far not the only part of your physiology to cycle in a circadian manner. Another important circadian variation is that of body temperature, the focus of today's chapter. Why is it important? The temperature of your body is surprisingly closely connected to sleep and alertness and is among the best predictors of when you will fall asleep or how tired you feel in the morning. Understanding temperature will give you a well-rounded understanding of why and how certain things support or hinder your way towards healthy morning energy. It will expand your toolset for rhythm advancement, but you will also find acute reactive measures for higher alertness in the morning.

Core body temperature (CBT)

Not all parts of your body are equally warm at a given time. Core body temperature describes the temperature of your body center, including your inner organs. Although core temperature itself varies throughout the day, it is more stable than the temperature in your extremities (arms or legs), which your body regulates differently in different (warm or cold) environments.

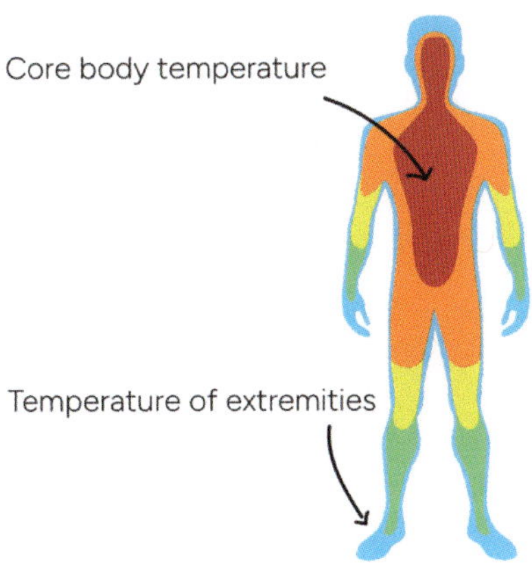

Like cortisol and melatonin, your core body temperature follows a circadian rhythm as well. Your core temperature increases before noon, reaches its peak in the afternoon, and then starts to decrease to reach its minimum during the night or early morning. The change amplitude is usually above 1.0°C/1.8°F throughout the day.

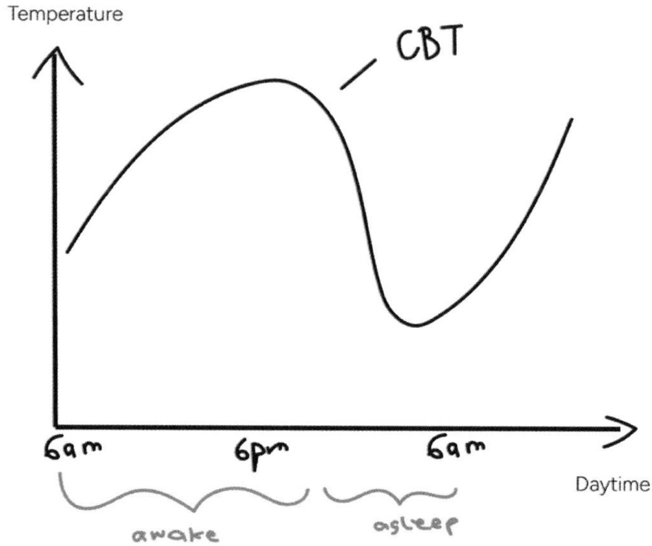

Like the starting point of melatonin release (referred to as *dim light melatonin onset*), core body temperature timing can be used to assess your circadian phase, i.e. how your circadian clock is set. With the respective tools (e.g. an ingestible probe that wirelessly transmits its readings), the core temperature can be continuously measured. This is convenient, as continuous measurement is currently not possible for melatonin rhythms.

The core temperature minimum is of particular interest for this matter. That is why it has got its own name in science: "*nadir*". Nadir is regarded as clock time "zero" regarding your circadian clock. It marks the turning point of how external stimuli shift your circadian clock. We already established that bright light in the evening delays your clock while morning light advances it. Your core temperature minimum marks the point where the direction is flipped.

Nadir occurs, on average, two hours before your habitual wake time, although this is really only an average. In reality, it can depend on different things, like the amount of social jet lag you have, i.e. your actual wake time compared to your natural wake time.

Broadly put, a higher core temperature correlates with alertness, while a lower core temperature is linked to relaxation. Your activities and environment can acutely influence your core temperature. This correlates with a change in alertness and, depending on when it is done, can even shift your circadian rhythm. But there is a temperature measure that is even more closely connected to sleepiness than core temperature alone: Your distal-proximal skin temperature gradient.

Distal-proximal skin temperature gradient (DPG)

Earlier in the chapter, I mentioned that your core temperature can differ from the temperature in your arms and legs. This difference in temperature is actually highly relevant when we look at sleep and wake-up. Let us quickly define the concept: "Distal-to-proximal skin temperature gradient" (DPG) is the difference in temperature, at any given point in time, between the skin temperature measured for hands or feet and the skin temperature measured at the body center. DPG throughout the day, on average, can range from around -4°C/-7.2°F ("wide", arm/feet cooler than core) around noon to 0°C/0°F) or even slightly above ("narrow", arm/feet similarly warm as core) during the night. This means that your body heat is more centralized during the day and evenly distributed at night, as shown in the following figure.

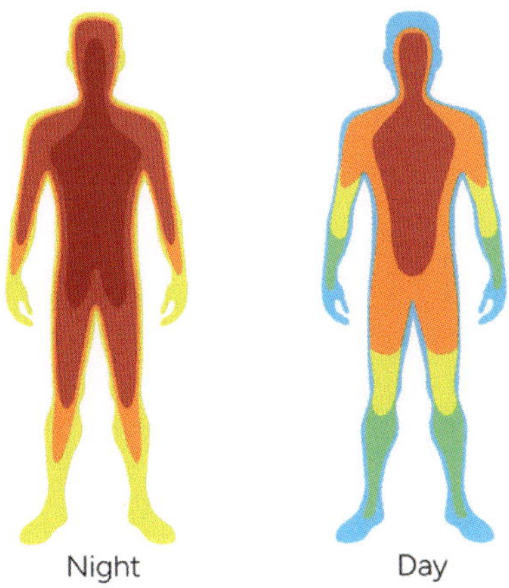

What researchers have found are two things:

- In the morning, the narrower your DPG, i.e. the more evenly distributed body temperature is, the more tired and dazed you feel[30].
- In the evening, sleep onset is connected to a strong narrowing of DPG (hands and feet getting warmer while the core is cooling down). The point in time of the strongest DPG increase in the evening has been shown to be the best predictor for sleep onset among a broad set of vital parameters (such as core temperature, heart rate, etc.)[31]: You typically fall asleep around the time your hands and feet are getting warmer.

Let us establish:

Distal-proximal Skin Temperature Gradient (DPG)		
wide DPG	centralized body heat, high core temperature	highly alert
narrow DPG	even heat distribution, low core temperature	sleepy

Would that mean that measures that affect your DPG also affect your sleepiness? The answer is yes. Let us find out how you can use that knowledge.

How to influence your body temperature

How different actions affect your body temperature can be a good proxy for how they affect your level of alertness. If so, how do previously discussed measures fit into that puzzle? Do bright light or caffeine widen DPG? It turns out they do[32,33]. What else can you do to make a difference?

Exercise

Movement is one of *the* contributors to a long and healthy life. Besides cardiovascular health (a healthy heart) and body composition, physical exercise yields significant positive effects on depression, comparable to antidepressant drugs (and can even help in combination with them)[34]. Furthermore, regular exercise has been found to be an effective preventive measure against Alzheimer's disease and other forms of dementia[35].

For our purposes, what we are interested in is the effect of exercise on body temperature as well as the circadian rhythm. Intense physical activity increases core body temperature (while your distal skin temperature may actually decrease). The higher the intensity, the more pronounced the effect. Also, longer duration increases the heating effect on core body temperature.

At the same time, high-intensity exercises increase blood flow in the brain and support the release of cortisol, which are both considered to support alertness in the morning, too. A study from 2021 found that 30 seconds of intense cycling right after awakening could already improve subjective alertness (but were not quite enough to raise core body temperature)[36].

While further research has yet to be conducted, 10-minute moderate-intensity exercise with some high-intensity elements, e.g. a 🔗 body-weight workout including jumps/burpees or a morning jog including some sprints, should be good enough to boost core temperature and, thereby, alertness and even cognitive performance in the morning. From an anecdotal perspective (my personal and peers' experience), this seems to be correct.

That said, your exercise routine may not only improve alertness in the moment but also for future mornings. If timed correctly, exercise is quite a potent zeitgeber, i.e. a stimulus to shift your circadian clock. In a study, one hour of moderate cardio exercise on a treadmill advanced the circadian phase for almost 1 hour when done in the morning or early afternoon[37]. On the other hand, it delayed the circadian clock for about one hour on average when performed in the evening[37]. The timing of your exercise, therefore, matters greatly for your inner clock. Counting 1+1 together, you may notice that morning exercise in daylight stacks the advantages of light and physical activity, paving the way for a great day and an earlier sleep-wake rhythm overall.

Like with morning light, the data point at larger shifts for longer exercise duration and higher intensity. Make use of this to maximize your results if you can and want to take time for extensive morning sports sessions. If not, dare to start small. If jumping around while listening to music is enough to get you out of breath, it qualifies as morning exercise! Keep in mind that your exercise routine should be something you want and can follow in the three upcoming mornings.

Daily: Exercise

Draft a 5+ min exercise protocol that you are motivated to follow in the morning, which includes elements of high intensity. Ideally, you can do it outdoors to benefit from morning daylight at the same time. Write it in your checklist. You can add it to your morning routine.

Be aware that at night, both the clock-delaying effects and acute heating (thus, alerting) effects of exercise may impair your ability to fall asleep. While low-intensity activities like soft yoga or stretching can support a good night's rest, try to avoid running or challenging workouts at night.

If you have fixed evening exercise hours because you pursue a team sport with late practice hours, for example, avoiding evening exercise may not be an option for you. In that case, just concentrate on the other measures to support your morningness and evening relaxation with even more diligence.

Daily: Evening rest

Do not exercise in the time window 2 h prior to your desired bed time. As a rule of thumb, your activity is too intense if it makes you sweat at room temperature. Write that in your checklist.

Cold showers

Cold air, cold showers or even ice baths - cold exposure is one of the favorite tools in the health enthusiast's toolbox, with data indicating mood-improving and immune-system-strengthening effects. Indeed, turning the water cold for at least the last 30 seconds of showering reduced sick leaves by 30% in a large Dutch study[38].

Regarding better mornings, cold showers provide two benefits: One is the body's acute "stress" reaction in response to the cold, with the hormone norepinephrine and increased blood flow supporting the body's natural self-activation in the first hour after awakening. Secondly, cold exposure increases metabolic heat production to counteract the danger of hypothermia (getting too cold). So, besides the centralization of temperature (cooler hands and feet), your core body temperature may actually increase after a cold shower: Higher core temperature, wide DPG - both boxes from this chapter are ticked. Alertness all the way!

The nice thing about cold showers is that they, like bright light exposure, can be coupled with a morning exercise routine. Prior exercise will make the thought of having a cold shower much more appealing.

Daily: Cold treatment

Finish your morning shower with cold water or shower cold, entirely (or feel free to use another form of cold exposure, if available). Write that in your checklist.

Note: To get the most out of the alerting effect, experts recommend 2-3 minutes of cold-water exposure[39]. That is quite long! Remember that habit formation is a journey, so you do not have to go all in right away. Maybe just start with the last few seconds of your shower time and work your way from there. Make sure you can be in warm enough clothes directly after. At the same time, keep in mind that the "stress" induced by cold water is actually healthy. This mindset may help you embrace the challenge and push yourself a bit further each day. Once you get used to it, you might even start enjoying it! And you may feel quite accomplished afterwards.

Evening Thermoregulation

Experts recommend your bedroom environment to be quite cool (around 18°C/65°F)[40,41]. Why is that? By now, you know that your body temperature decreases towards the night and sleep onset is linked to a strong narrowing in DPG (i.e. your hands and feet get warmer while your core temperature drops). To get your body ready for sleep, you want to give it the chance to cool down and dissipate heat. If your bedroom is cool, you can keep your feet under the blanket and still have enough skin surface area with your head and maybe hands to dissipate heat to the environment. If that does not suffice, you may be familiar with the urge to stick one or two legs out of the blanket to give your body more skin area to dissipate heat. If that still does not suffice, you will feel hot and uncomfortable, and your sleep may be compromised. If, before bedtime, your core temperature is too high (e.g. due to exercise in the evening), a lukewarm to warm shower or bath may help the body dissipate heat more effectively.[42]

On the other hand, you do not want to feel *too* cold at night! If your room is cold and your blanket is too thin, your body will keep its temperature centralized, afraid of hypothermia. This can make it hard to fall asleep. Cold feet at night may be an indicator of this. In this case, taking the measures to feel warm enough is a good idea. Evidence shows that a warm bath just for the feet before bedtime or wearing socks at night can help you fall asleep faster[43,44].

Note: If temperature has been a lasting issue for your sleep, you may want to consider further help from products like thermo-regulating pillows or mattress covers. Find our list of useful tools for thermo-regulation in the tools section on our 🔗 website.

Summary Chapter 4: Remember this

- Your core body temperature follows a circadian variation. It increases in the morning and decreases in the evening.
- The temperature gradient between the extremities and body core (DPG) correlates with your sleepiness. Actions to acutely widen your DPG can acutely increase your alertness.
- Exercise in the morning can boost alertness and advance your circadian clock. Evening exercise can delay your clock and make falling asleep more difficult.
- Cold showers are another good way to boost morning alertness healthily.
- Sleep in a cool environment, but make sure you do not feel too cold.

Resources Chapter 4: Scan to follow the 🔗 links

Here are some suggestions for exercises we like to do:
www.love-mornings.com/tools/exercises

Recommendations and more information on thermo-regulation duvets, mattresses & more:
www.love-mornings.com/tools/thermo

Day 5: Nutrition and substance intake

Welcome to day 5! Today, we will look at the role that your eating habits can play in loving mornings. Spoiler: In the end, I will recommend you to not eat in the last 2 - 3 hours before bedtime. Why? This is not as straightforward as one may think. So let us have a look!

Eating and chronotype

Like many processes in your body, your metabolism underlies a circadian rhythm. This means there is a cyclic daily variation in, for example, your blood glucose levels or how your body responds to food intake across the day. Some elements of this variation are quite malleable: You can *entrain* digestive activity levels to match your preferred meal schedule if you eat roughly at the same time every day. Maybe you know the feeling of getting hungry right before lunchtime? This is not just psychological: It has been shown that digestion-related processes experience a peak in anticipation of a large meal at a specific, entrained time of day[45].

Interestingly, it seems that this metabolic clock can work largely uncoupled from your sleep-wake rhythm. What does that mean? You can entrain the mentioned digestive peaks to happen at a time of your choice. It can be any time of day, irrespective of your sleep-wake rhythm, as long as you stay consistent. This uncoupling also means that eating late does not necessarily translate to becoming more of a night owl, as a recent study has shown: Cortisol and melatonin rhythms were unaffected by a 6-hour delay in meal timing[46]. Why would experts then still recommend fasting before bedtime?

1. Late eating poses a risk to sleep hygiene

In the broad population, late eating is associated with worse health[47]. Even though a late versus early dinner does not cause critical changes in sleep architecture per se[48], there are reasonable explanations why late dinners can be problematic:

- Sleeping on a full stomach can be a barrier to nighttime recovery[47]. If you have ever had acid reflux, you will know how directly food can impair your sleep. Yet, even if you can fall asleep well, your body cannot fully focus on sleep processes but needs to do digestive work, too. This may be reflected in a higher heart rate and worse subjective sleep quality.
- Eating is usually not an isolated process. It is often accompanied by light and cognitive stimulation, which are both alerting factors. Moreover, eating before bedtime may interfere with your wind-down routine. Remember that you will entrain yourself to be hungry late if eating late is a habit: Even if you are tired, you may have a hard time going to sleep early when your hunger kicks in and leaves you lying in bed dissatisfied.

2. Time-restricted eating is healthy

As much as you can entrain your metabolic clock with regular meal timing, you can also disrupt it with irregular meal timing. This leads to energy bursts and health problems and is associated with weight gain and high blood pressure[49]. Giving your digestive tract enough off-time seems to be of particular importance. Did you know that the average person eats seven times a day?[50] In addition to meals, snacking is a thing that keeps our guts busy.

Fasting has been shown to be good for health. Not just when you want to lose weight, fasting can lead to healthier blood pressure and insulin resistance levels[51]. Fasting is, at least in mice, a factor for longevity[52]. In the "16-8" intermittent fasting schedule, you limit your food intake to a consistent time window of consecutive 8 hours of your day and abstain from food (and sugary/caloric drinks) during the other 16 hours. This is a great help for your metabolic circadian clock, as your gut will know precisely when to be active and when to rest.

A study with mice from 2012 demonstrated the power of "16-8" fasting[53]: One group of mice was given a high-fat and carb diet with unlimited access to the food. Another group could eat the same food but only during 8 hours of the day. Even though the mice consumed the same total amount of calories, mice in the constant access group ended up weighing almost twice as much as the mice with the 8-hour eating window!

The latter remained healthy and did not weigh much more than a third group that was given healthy food[53]. This kind of intermittent fasting (that takes circadian rhythm into account) is called *time-restricted eating* (TRE). TRE has shown health benefits in humans, too[51]. Interestingly, while it can help with losing excess weight, TRE does not hinder athletes from building muscle[54]. Hence, even if you have an active lifestyle, it may be worth considering.

However, not every individual does well with 16 hours of fasting each day. Anything up to a 12:12 ratio is considered time-restricted. According to chrono-nutrition researcher Satchin Panda, twelve hours of fasting is still more than 90% of the Western population do[50]. With regards to the time window for eating, emerging evidence indicates that early TRE schedules may be even more beneficial than late TRE schedules[55]. If you aim to give your body some healthy fasting time, you will not want to eat too late in the evening.

Be aware that your body needs time to re-entrain to your new pattern. "I'm just so hungry in the evening/not hungry in the morning" may well be accurate at the spoken time, but hunger timing is eventually under your control. Give your body some time before making a judgment.

Daily: No late food

Finish your latest meal 1 - 3 h before bedtime. If you currently have the habit of eating late, choose a shorter duration to avoid strong hunger at bedtime. Feel free to increase the duration over time. Water or herbal tea (no sugar/no milk) are okay during your fast.

Alcohol

Alcohol is frequently used to induce relaxation and sleep[56]. In addition to its sedative effects on the nervous system, alcohol widens the blood vessels in your arms and legs. This leads to your hands and feet getting warmer. With your knowledge of thermoregulation, you may see how alcohol's link to sleepiness, too, is consistent with the DPG model presented in Chapter 4. Indeed, independent of dose, alcohol shortens sleep onset latency, which is the time it takes you to fall asleep[57]. However, while these effects seem appealing, the harmful effects of alcohol on sleep (→ less restorative[58]) and overall health make avoiding alcohol the recommended option. You have already learned about healthier ways to increase nighttime sleepiness. I encourage you not to consume alcohol until the end of the course to make the most out of the sleep you get.

Melatonin

Melatonin plays a vital role in the regulation of your sleep-wake cycle. While your body produces melatonin itself, it can also be added from the outside in the form of supplements. Melatonin supplements do not require a medical prescription and are available as over-the-counter drugs in most countries.

Can you really influence your level of tiredness or even your circadian rhythm with supplemented melatonin? Yes, you can. Because of this, melatonin is becoming increasingly popular as a sleep aid. Moreover, melatonin is likely the second most potent "zeitgeber" after light: In a lab setting, melatonin taken at the right time over three days advanced participants' circadian clock by over one hour on average[59]. Further studies indicate that the effect of melatonin can be stacked with those of morning bright light[60]. For *delayed sleep phase disorder* (DSPD), an extreme form of being a night owl, combining light therapy and melatonin supplementation is a popular treatment approach[61].

Should you take melatonin, then? This is not a question I can answer for you. Before you start tampering with it, be aware that melatonin is a hormone. It plays a functional role in puberty in humans. In rodents, increased melatonin levels are associated with hibernation and cause significant changes in physiology. This book aims to provide healthy advice. So far, the presented interventions are not only helpful in advancing your rhythm but they are all known to be inherently healthy. With melatonin, we cross that line. According to a scientific review from 2016, the short-term use of melatonin is considered safe (except for pregnant or breastfeeding women, due to a lack of studies there)[62]. Long-term melatonin supplementation for children or adolescents requires further investigation. When in doubt, please inform yourself about potential side effects and consult a doctor to make an informed decision.

If you do decide to take melatonin, there are two things I would like you to know:

- For sleep, many people take melatonin about 1.5 hours before bedtime. This is fair to help with sleep but will have little effect on your circadian rhythm. If you want to advance your rhythm, a study has shown that melatonin is most potent when taken much earlier[59]. When 0.5 mg of melatonin was used, intake timing for maximal effect was 3.3 h before the natural onset of melatonin, which translates to 5 h before habitual bedtime[59].
- Above 0.5 mg, a greater melatonin dose does not seem to yield greater circadian phase shifts. In the aforementioned study, 3 mg of melatonin led to the same average circadian phase advance (1.5 hours) as 0.5 mg. The difference was that the 3 mg supplement had to be taken even earlier for maximum effect, about 7 hours before bedtime.[59]

A recent investigation showed that in many melatonin supplements, the actual dose deviated strongly from the information on the label[63]. If you choose to use melatonin, please ensure you get a 🔗 reliable product.

Other supplements

There are a bunch of supplements out there that promise better sleep and, consequently, a feeling of being refreshed the following morning. What does science say? A meta-study from 2021 considered melatonin, Vitamin D and some amino acids as the only supplements sufficiently studied to say they mostly help with sleep[64]. This does not necessarily mean that other supplements cannot be helpful: magnesium and apigenin (the active ingredient in chamomile) repeatedly get praised by science influencer Andrew Huberman[5]. Those praises are backed by studies, but the number of studies is still low.

My take on supplements is this: If you have got deficits, e.g. of Vitamin D or magnesium, supplementation clearly makes sense and can make a big difference. If you choose to explore supplementation beyond that, please inform yourself about timing, dosage and possible side effects (some commonly advertised substances can be psychoactive and cause nightmares or diarrhea). Feel free to do what may help you. However, please do not mistake supplements for an alternative to a healthy lifestyle. Supplements are among the most profitable products sold to health-aware people. This is likely reflected in supplements being overly promoted, compared to effective but non-monetizable lifestyle interventions (e.g. exercise or daylight exposure). No supplement is an excuse for ignoring the effective lifestyle basics.

Summary Chapter 5: Remember this

- Your metabolism follows its own circadian rhythm. Regular meal times can help entrain a healthy metabolic rhythm with digestive peaks at the time of food intake.
- Eating late at night can impair your sleep, as the body has to focus on digestion instead of rest. Try to finish your last meal 2-3 hours before bedtime.
- Time-restricted eating, notably on a "16-8" schedule, has been shown to be beneficial for health. It means you limit your daily calorie intake to a consistent 8-hour window and fast for the rest.
- Alcohol can help induce sleep, but its detrimental effects on sleep quality and overall health outweigh its benefits.
- Melatonin supplements can influence tiredness and the circadian rhythm. However, they should be used with caution due to their hormonal nature and potential side effects.
- Supplements shall not substitute for a healthy lifestyle.

Resources Chapter 5: Scan to follow the 🔗 links

Recommendations and further information on melatonin & other supplements:
www.love-mornings.com/tools/supplements

Wow.
Day 6 already!

Day 6: Staying consistent

Imagine a child on a swing. The child wants to get the best out of their ride and asks you to help. How would you push the child to gain speed and a high amplitude? Most likely you would start slowly: push, wait, push, wait. Your push would gradually become stronger, but still, the pattern stays: push, wait, push, wait. If you push too early, you might stop the kid, as it might still be on the way towards you. Importantly, once the child has reached an amplitude that is fun, you maintain the amplitude by giving it your push in the same rhythm.

This analogy by German photobiologist Alexander Wunsch[65] beautifully illustrates how the consistent timing of zeitgebers, especially light, contributes to a healthy circadian rhythm. The forward swing is your daytime energy; the backward swing is your sleep.

You will want to push your "circadian child" with morning light right after the turn (which is the core temperature minimum, also known as *nadir*), right when it is about to catch speed again, and let it sleep deeply in its backward swing. Small incentives may suffice to keep the amplitude, as long as they are timed consistently. If you push before the turn, you will rapidly slow the child down. If you do nothing, its speed will slowly but eventually fade.

Intuitive as well, what happens when you make random pushes, i.e. sleep and expose yourself to light at irregular intervals? Exactly, the ride will suck! And your circadian child will not be happy. Bringing it back to speed will cost a lot of effort every time you disrupt the flow.

Consistency is key

In his bestseller "Why We Sleep", sleep researcher Matthew Walker lists "keeping a consistent sleep schedule" as his number one advice for a better nighttime rest[4]. A study from 2023 indicates that to improve quality of life, consistency in *when* you sleep is just as important as *how long* you sleep[66]. Furthermore, interestingly, a study from 2013 found that sleep timing was the best predictor for exam performance among medical school students, more predictive than sleep duration or even sleep quality. Earlier schedules performed better, independent of chronotype[67].

What about the other side of the coin? Inconsistent schedules negatively impact your circadian stability and thereby everything connected to it. In mice, lighting schedules that disrupt circadian rhythms were shown to evoke symptoms of depression and impaired memory *within days*[68]. More than that, chronic jet lag (induced by disruptive light-dark cycles) led old mice to die earlier than the control group[69].

In humans, shift work has been shown to increase the risk for depression[70], and even a single night shift was enough to impair healthy adolescents' mood in an experiment[71]. Conversely, an appropriately timed bright light schedule has been shown to help shift workers maintain a better mood. Consistent early-morning bright light exposure is a first-line treatment for seasonal affective disorder (S.A.D., also known as "winter depression")[72]. It is also significantly effective in the treatment of unipolar depression[73] or antepartum depression[74].

So let us stay consistent, should we not? This is much easier said than done! Our daily life offers a lot of incentive to break the steady pattern. Before we declare pre-maturely “how things ought to be”, it is of vital importance to understand why people stay up late and acknowledge the needs that are satisfied by breaking the early bird’s pattern. Only then, we can try to work out ways to align a fulfilled life with a consistent, morning-friendly schedule.

On evening me-time

Earlier in this book, I set the premise that whether you will get up early in the morning depends on whether the expected reward of doing so outweighs the expected reward of staying in bed. To create a lasting lifestyle, though, we need to expand the scope a little further. This leads us to the complete premise of this book:

To be a healthy early riser sustainably, your expected reward of rising as well as of going to sleep early must typically outweigh the expected reward of rising and staying up late.

It is important to include going to sleep early – if you do not, you will compromise your enjoyment of mornings and their health benefits over time. An increasing sleep debt will make your journey unsustainable.

The biological reason behind going to sleep late – just not being tired – has already been addressed in earlier chapters and helpful measures have been presented. But there is more to it than just biology: For many people, evenings represent quality time. Having done all the chores of the day, the evening finally awaits you with undisturbed me-time to enjoy. Our culture fosters this attitude, which I want to introduce as the *eveningness paradigm*. It is the world view that "pleasurable times come after work", usually in the evening. Pleasurable times can be a movie night, a fine wine with friends, the pursuit of a personal project or even just doom-scrolling on TikTok for hours. The evening, after all, represents time that you owe nobody but yourself. Cutting this time short by going to bed early may feel like depriving yourself of a vital part that makes life worth living... and it gets worse if you associate the next morning with nothing but to-dos!

The reluctancy to go to bed when evenings represent the one source of quality time has reached a level that it has got its own name: *Revenge bedtime procrastination* describes the sacrifice of nighttime sleep for me-time and is a prevalent phenomenon in society[75]. While the negative consequences for the next day are rationally clear, revenge bedtime procrastination illustrates the (very human) need to (over-)compensate for an overwhelming day with extensive me-time at night.

With our book, we want to help you live your most fulfilled life. While productivity may be one means to this end, I invite you to take your human need for re-creation seriously in your planning. In addition to simply making your life more enjoyable, a self-compassionate lifestyle is much more likely to be maintained sustainably.

How can we go about this? We have established that self-determined quality time is important. Yet, the evening paradigm comes with a catch: Self-determination can be a slippery slope! When analyzing evening me-time, how much of what we do is what we really consider fulfilling? Perhaps you are very intentional about how you spend your evenings. If, on the other hand, you often find yourself carried away doing things you would consider a waste of time in retrospect, this does not come by coincidence. When it comes to self-control, evenings represent a sensitive time of day:

- Your energy and willpower have been depleted throughout your day.
- For the rest of the day, you face no further externally dictated restraint.

This is a fertile ground for distractions and impulsive behaviors. Couple this with the use of modern media, which are designed to keep your attention. Staying in control of your actions can quickly become an uphill battle.

A recently published study with people from Finland connects the evening chronotype with a higher mortality than the morning type[76]. Interestingly, the cause does not seem to lie in chronotype per se, but in more unhealthy behavior (e.g. smoking, drinking) exhibited by evening types. An increased tendency for impulsive behaviors and insufficient sleep due to the reasons mentions above may be one explanation for this.

Again, there are many great things to spend your evenings on. The holy grail of quality time, just like with any other part of the day, is being intentional about your actions.

The morningness paradigm

I would like to propose to you a rule of thumb for being intentional about me-time activities in the evening. What do you really consider worthwhile? To evaluate candidates, ask yourself: Would you want to get out of bed for this in the morning? If the answer is no, you may only do this activity because it is entertaining, stimulating or easy to do in the evening. Considering an activity for the morning is a much tougher criterion for an activity to be worthwhile. Yet, whether you do things in the evening or in the morning, they take the same amount of time and sleep from you.

As a next step, I invite you to consider actually doing me-time activities in the morning. With this, I would like to propose the *morningness paradigm*: It is the world view that spending quality time in the morning is not only okay but can actually be beneficial for your entire day. Starting your day with me-time can help you get out of bed easier, set a positive mood for the day and thereby even contribute to more productivity during work. Tranquil mornings, when compared with the risks of evening me-time, have properties that can set the stage for activities that you truly deem fulfilling:

- In the morning, no other activity has yet depleted your willpower for the day.
- Fixed dates later in the morning (e.g. work times) help you stick to your intended schedule and not exceed your time limits.

If your intended activities require cognitive effort (like the work on a personal project), the morningness paradigm can increase your odds of really doing them. But even if it is not about effort, starting the day with something you like is a self-compassionate act. When, later, there is a lot of work to do during the day, your chores will not have compromised your fair share of me-time. Lastly, getting up at a self-determined time, in contrast to "when you have to", can award you with a downright amazing feeling of being in control of your life.

If your mornings become your source of me-time, the evenings can become a source of true relaxation. It can be incredibly gratifying to go to bed early, maybe after a bath, a book or some 🔗 easy yoga - if you have accumulated sleep debt from the week, even more so! But even without sleep debt, everything I have said so far aims at making you tired more consistently in the evening. Let your evening tiredness serve you as a reminder of what you truly want.

To Do: Reflection

Make a list of your typical evening activities and evaluate them by whether they would be worth standing up for. Cross out the things that are not. Add activities that you would definitely find worthwhile. Label each item whether it would qualify as an evening and/or a morning activity. If your results affect what you want your routines to be, make suitable adjustments.

Evenings as social time

Finally, there are occasions where your evening schedule is not under your control but set by friends you want to spend time with, or by public events. We have dedicated to this case a separate chapter "Cheat Days", which you find as a supplement chapter later in this book. Please continue there to finish your Day 6.

Summary Chapter 6: Remember this

- Your circadian rhythm is healthy if it consistently gets the right stimuli at the right time.
- A consistent sleep schedule is similarly important as a long enough sleep duration. Chronic disruptions not only impair your daytime energy but also pose a long-term health risk.
- To be a healthy early riser, it is critical to go to bed early, too. The *eveningness paradigm*, where pleasurable times come after work, can make early bedtimes feel unfulfilling.
- In the *morningness paradigm*, quality time in the morning is viewed as a facilitator for a good day. Moving me-time from evening to morning can make the start of the day much more appealing.
- To be intentional about how you spend your evenings, ask yourself whether a given activity would be worth getting up for in the morning. Whatever the timing, it costs the same amount of sleep.

Resources Chapter 6: Scan to follow the 🔗 links

Here are some suggestions for exercises we like to do:
www.love-mornings.com/tools/exercises

Day 7: Your future as an early riser

It is Day 7. Congratulations on making it here! If you have followed the tasks diligently, we hope you have gotten a glimpse of what mornings can be for you. How did it feel? How did it work for you? Maybe you have made it to waking up even before your alarm. Maybe it was hard to really comply with the tasks. Maybe the temptations of the eveningness paradigm were still prevalent. Maybe you felt like finding yourself in an otherwise distracted world: Maybe some things felt weird as they deviated from cultural norms.

This course's aim is not to set your new lifestyle but to show you how you can do it yourself. When I first implemented all the tasks for myself, I found them to be very effective, but it was hard to maintain the lifestyle over time. It is just so easy to drift away from it, with impaired compliance leading to impaired results, making it ever more difficult to get back on track. It is like with nutrition or fitness; circadian health takes some discipline and repeated effort.

Looking into the future, how could you turn your knowledge into a sustainable lifestyle? I want to give you the following advice on your way:

Environment

When it comes to circadian health, you have one great advantage over healthy nutrition or fitness: Light as the dominant factor (and also temperature to some extent) is an environmental stimulus. Smart Light Technologies supporting "circadian lighting", sunrise alarm clocks, a daylight lamp or simply candles available at the right place can greatly help you get the right light at the right time. Adjusting your environment to automatically support your circadian health takes effort once but provides sustained benefits for your daily life.

Note: To find the tools we use ourselves, as well as further recommendations, visit the tools section on our 🔗 website.

Culture

Throughout the course, you may already have found yourself in the position that you know more about circadian health than people around you. This will continue into the future: Lighting conditions in restaurants, schools, work, or other people's homes are often far from what is scientifically recommended. The timing of social events you get invited to may be counterproductive for circadian health, too. This can get quite frustrating. I invite you to try to make a difference. Instead of going to a bar with a friend at night, suggest having breakfast or going on a morning walk at the weekend. Think of possibilities and suggest them to your friends. Lead by example. Share with other people what you found insightful about this topic. Having your partner/family/people you live with on board is the most effective place to start. You may inspire others and even improve their lives while making the maintenance of your personal health easier.

Habit

What timeline can you really expect when trying to adopt new habits? It is not seven days; it is not the commonly communicated 21 days. It takes, on average, 65 days until behaviors become automated habits (and it can be more or less, depending on the complexity of the task)[77]. This was recently addressed in the blog of James Clear, author of "Atomic Habits"[78]. If you have benefited from this course, you have laid the ideal foundation, but there is yet a way to go until your desired actions become a lasting part of your life. Remember that your plan is only as good as your compliance. Thus, as the last exercises of this course, take the time to review your checklist and routines: Make them suitable for a longer-term implementation.

Only what gets measured gets managed: To help establish a habit, we have made the experience that keeping track of your actions makes compliance much more likely. If you liked the checklist provided with the course, you can find a downloadable PDF for further use, as well as other tracking options, under the 🔗 link at the end of this chapter. This includes our dedicated "Love Mornings Habit Tracker" booklet, which provides a checklist template for 100 days.

To assist with desired lifestyle changes beyond habit tracking, we also collect other resources and have even created our own: Find our 🔗 "5 min for me" 5-minute journal for daily scribbles. We tried a lot of journals and distilled the most helpful parts into that book. It helps us practice gratitude most effectively and may help you do the same.

☐ To Do: Future routine redraw

Schedule a time in approximately one week in your calendar to redraw your morning and evening routines. Make them suitable for long-term execution. Let them be rewarding, be good to yourself! Take your routines sheet and pin it somewhere where you have it visible. If you got to a result that feels right, you are done.

☐ To Do: Checklist review

Review your checklist from this course. Feel free to make changes to the time limits or even cut some of the points that you do not see yourself implementing (considering that any cut will come at a cost of efficacy). Make your goal to find a set of rules that you think you will be able and want to implement for good. Take your revised checklist and, if it is the 🔗 printed version, pin it somewhere where you have them visible, to be reminded of your goals and your why.

Congratulations!

If you have one, tell your accountability buddy that you have made it through the course (and pay eventual debts) 🙄 You're a free elf!

Whatever it is you make out of it, we hope to have given you the knowledge, tools and experiences to make informed and self-determined choices for your future. Ultimately, it is about living your life the way you want. We hope our book can serve you as an enabler on this journey.

I hope you enjoyed this book and make the most of what you have learned. In the name of my entire team, I wish you all the best!

Note: We invite you to join the *love mornings* community. Discuss the science, ask questions, share your stories & results, give feedback and exchange thoughts with like-minded people. Become part of the science-based movement towards better circadian health in society. Find us on Reddit under 🔗 r/lovemornings.

Summary Chapter 7: Remember this

- Sustaining your circadian health takes repeated action. To make it a part of your life, integrate your newly gained knowledge into your lifestyle.
- Changes to the environment take effort once but can provide long-term benefits. Smart light technologies or a sunrise alarm clock can passively support your health day by day.
- The behavior of people close to you will influence your own behavior. Invite others into the *love morning* lifestyle, e.g. by having breakfast instead of dinner together, or sharing your knowledge.
- Forming a habit takes time. Select the actions from your checklist that you want to adopt as habits for the future and revise your routines to suit your needs in the long term.
- Feel free to use our resources to keep track of your progress. Make use of our community channels to stay in touch.

Resources Chapter 7: Scan to follow the 🔗 links

Recommendations and further information on the tools we use & more:
www.love-mornings.com/tools

All resources and tracking options for this course, including a dedicated "Love Mornings Habit Tracker" booklet:
www.love-mornings.com/coursematerials#day7

Join our reddit community to discuss related topics, ask questions or get to know like-minded people (us included):
www.reddit.com/r/lovemornings

Don't we
all cheat
sometimes?

Extra: Cheat days

Even if you want it, staying consistent can still be hard! There may be that one party on the weekend, that movie you want to watch in the cinema... A steady rhythm means aiming for the same sleep and wake times seven days a week. You will feel fantastic if you do live accordingly, but there are legitimate reasons to break the pattern occasionally. Attending social events to foster social connections, for example, is definitely something that can make life overall more fulfilling. It is fair not to want to isolate yourself from all your surroundings for your circadian health.
What can you do when you anticipate a very late bedtime? To keep your balance, keep as many dimensions of your schedule consistent as you can, despite disrupting others. If you are out for the night, you may go to sleep much later than usual that night. But you may have the chance to stay consistent with:

- **Your eating schedule**: If you do not eat after 8 p.m. on regular days, have a good dinner that night but not a midnight snack. Your digestive system has a circadian rhythm, too, so try to keep it steady. A study from 2022 indicates that consistent eating times despite shift work may lower health risks usually connected with shift work.
- **Smartphone stimulation**: Apart from the smartphone interaction that you need to survive the night out, stick to your no-screen policy. Checking your phone can be really tempting when you are on your way home, but the evidence makes clear that not using your smartphone is the healthier option. In my personal experience, the difference it makes can be vast.
- Most importantly: **Your lighting schedule**. Data indicate it may be the aberrant light timing rather than the disruption in your sleep-wake schedule that disrupts your circadian clock[79]. Take it as an opportunity! How could you maintain your lighting schedule even on cheat days?

- If you use a wake-up light or smart lighting to wake up with, set the artificial dawn to happen at your regular wake time, despite your night out. If you usually sleep with open blinds or curtains, do so after your night out, too. Even if your eyes are closed, your brain will notice the dawn signal through the eyelids, and you will be able to maintain your rhythm more easily. If you cannot sleep through the light, turn your lights off or close the blinds once you have woken up. Go back to sleep if you feel like you need to.
- *Experimental*: If you come home late and have no appointments the next day, do *still* get up at your usual wake time. Get up, get dressed, have a 10-minute daylight walk outside and, optionally, shower. Go back to sleep. If you have got way too little sleep until then, chances are you will be tired enough to fall back asleep. Still, you have given your circadian system a strong cue to help maintain its rhythm. This method works really well for me, personally (it actually feels wonderful, giving in to the urge for more sleep while being freshly showered). However, not everybody may be able to fall asleep again. In that case, you may consider spending the morning awake and use the natural energy dip after lunch for a nap. Reward yourself with a very early bedtime the following night.

  Heads up here: I do not know of scientific studies investigating this approach, so this is just anecdotal. Given what I know, I do think it makes sense, and it is the most effective way I personally found to deal with the issue. Yet, take it with a grain of salt and take your needed sleep duration seriously in your consideration. Let us know in our Reddit community 🔗 *r/lovemornings* how this approach works for you.
- On your way home from the event, wear blue light-blocking glasses (as long as this doesn't compromise your safety in any way). If you do not own blue light blockers, simple sunglasses can help as well. If you are really committed and ready for discussions on circadian health, wear them even at the event itself.

- **Physical Exercise**: If you get up in the morning to get some light, consider adding some exercise. A morning jog after a night out can be quite a game-changer for the day to come. Furthermore, it strengthens the proper circadian cues you want to set.

To Do: Contract

Review and complete the contract you want to have with yourself regarding your next nights out and sign it.

Remember that disruptions, may it just be one day, can affect your circadian system and everything connected to it for much longer than just that. Did you know that "just" the one-hour time shift for daylight saving time lets the number of heart attacks rise by 25% on the Monday after[80]? It measurably takes night owls over one week to adapt to the change[81].

It is in your best interest to minimize disruptions as well as you can. Make use of your acquired knowledge to find your best set of tools to approach obstacles.

Cheat Days Contract

Nutrition:

No food after

Smartphone:

No unnecessary phone use after

Lighting:

(Which) Light exposure the next day?

Exercise:

(Which) Exercise to pursue the next day?

Signature

Resources Cheat Days: Scan to follow the 🔗 links

Join our reddit community to discuss related topics, ask questions or get to know like-minded people (us included): *www.reddit.com/r/lovemornings*

Resources: Recommended further reading

Introduction

- **Lifestyle adjustments for an earlier rhythm can bear multiple positive effects:**
  Facer-Childs, E. R., Middleton, B., Skene, D. J., & Bagshaw, A. P. (2019). Resetting the late timing of 'night owls' has a positive impact on mental health and performance. *Sleep Medicine, 60,* 236–247. https://doi.org/10.1016/J.SLEEP.2019.05.001
- **Foundations of "sleep inertia", i.e., morning tiredness:**
  Trotti, L. M. Waking up is the hardest thing I do all day: Sleep inertia and sleep drunkenness. Sleep Medicine Reviews 35, 76–84 (2017).

Day 1: Do no harm

- **Sleep pressure & circadian rhythm: The model of sleep regulation:**
  Borbély, A. A., Daan, S., Wirz-Justice, A., & Deboer, T. (2016). The two-process model of sleep regulation: A reappraisal. *Journal of Sleep Research, 25*(2), 131–143. https://doi.org/10.1111/jsr.12371
- **A good overview of the effects of light on human physiology:**
  Blume, C., Garbazza, C. & Spitschan, M. Effects of light on human circadian rhythms, sleep and mood. Somnologie 23, 147–156 (2019).
- **Expert lighting recommendations with regard to human health:**
  Brown, T. M., Brainard, G. C., Cajochen, C., Czeisler, C. A., Hanifin, J. P., Lockley, S. W., Lucas, R. J., Münch, M., O'Hagan, J. B., Peirson, S. N., Price, L. L. A., Roenneberg, T., Schlangen, L. J. M., Skene, D. J., Spitschan, M., Vetter, C., Zee, P. C., & Jr, K. P. W. (2022). Recommendations for daytime, evening, and nighttime indoor light exposure to best support physiology, sleep, and wakefulness in healthy adults. *PLOS Biology, 20*(3), e3001571. https://doi.org/10.1371/journal.pbio.3001571

- **Blue light blockers' effects on sleep:**
  Kimberly, B., & James R., P. (2009). Amber lenses to block blue light and improve sleep: A randomized trial. *Chronobiology International, 26*(8), 1602–1612. https://doi.org/10.3109/07420520903523719
- **Caffeine and adenosine:**
  Reichert, C. F., Deboer, T., & Landolt, H.-P. (2022). Adenosine, caffeine, and sleep-wake regulation: State of the science and perspectives. *Journal of Sleep Research, 31*(4), e13597. https://doi.org/10.1111/jsr.13597

Day 2: Circadian rhythm

- **Awakening during biological night leads to more sleep inertia:**
  Scheer, F. A. J. L., Shea, T. J., Hilton, M. F., & Shea, S. A. (2008). An endogenous circadian rhythm in sleep inertia results in greatest cognitive impairment upon awakening during the biological night. *Journal of Biological Rhythms, 23*(4), 353–361. https://doi.org/10.1177/0748730408318081
- **Chronotype distribution in society and social jet lag:**
  Roenneberg, Pilz, Zerbini, & Winnebeck. (2019). Chronotype and Social Jetlag: A (Self-) Critical Review. *Biology, 8*(3), 54. https://doi.org/10.3390/biology8030054
- **On the most sensitive times to shift circadian rhythm with light:**
  Khalsa, S. B. S., Jewett, M. E., Cajochen, C., & Czeisler, C. A. (2003). A phase response curve to single bright light pulses in human subjects. *Journal of Physiology, 549*(3), 945–952. https://doi.org/10.1113/jphysiol.2003.040477
- **One week of camping advances the circadian clock of night owls:**
  Wright, K. P., McHill, A. W., Birks, B. R., Griffin, B. R., Rusterholz, T., & Chinoy, E. D. (2013). Entrainment of the human circadian clock to the natural light-dark cycle. *Current Biology: CB, 23*(16), 1554–1558. https://doi.org/10.1016/j.cub.2013.06.039

Day 3: Routines

- **How to connect the morning with pleasant feelings:**
  Uyama, S. (2015): How To Love Waking Up: A Hands-On Guide

To Becoming A Morning Person, CreateSpace Independent Publishing Platform

- **Why some things keep you engaged and others do not**:
  Eyal, N, Hoover, Ryan. (2014). Hooked: how to build habit-forming products. New York: Portfolio Penguin.
- **Inspiration for your morning routine:**
  Elrod, H. The Miracle Morning: The Not-so-obvious Secret Guaranteed to Transform Your Life Before 8 AM. (Hal Elrod International, Incorporated, 2012).
- **The bestseller on building healthy habits**:
  Clear, J. (2018). *Atomic habits: tiny changes, remarkable results : an easy & proven way to build good habits & break bad ones.* New York, New York, Avery, an imprint of Penguin Random House.

Day 4: Body temperature

- **On the link between DPG and sleepiness in the morning:**
  Kräuchi, K., Cajochen, C., & Wirz-Justice, A. (2004). Waking up properly: Is there a role of thermoregulation in sleep inertia? *Journal of Sleep Research, 13*(2), 121–127. https://doi.org/10.1111/j.1365-2869.2004.00398.x
- **Dawn simulation accelerates the decline of DPG in the morning**:
  Giménez, M. C., Hessels, M., Van De Werken, M., De Vries, B., Beersma, D. G. M., & Gordijn, M. C. M. (2010). Effects of artificial dawn on subjective ratings of sleep inertia and dim light melatonin onset. *Chronobiology International, 27*(6), 1219–1241. https://doi.org/10.3109/07420528.2010.496912
- **Acute reactive measures against sleepiness in the morning:**
  Hilditch, C. J., Dorrian, J. & Banks, S. Time to wake up: Reactive countermeasures to sleep inertia. Industrial Health 54, 528–541 (2016).
- **The "when" of exercise and its effect on circadian rhythm**:
  Youngstedt, S. D., Elliott, J. A., & Kripke, D. F. (2019). Human circadian phase-response curves for exercise. *The Journal of Physiology, 597*(8), 2253–2268. https://doi.org/10.1113/JP276943

Day 5: Nutrition

- **Metabolic rhythm and sleep-wake rhythm can be uncoupled:**
  Vetter, C. & Scheer, F. A. J. L. Circadian Biology: Uncoupling Human Body Clocks by Food Timing. Current Biology 27, R656–R658 (2017).
- **An entire book with focus on time-restricted eating:**
  Panda, S. (2020). The circadian code: lose weight, supercharge your energy, and transform your health from morning to midnight. Rodale Books.
- **Time-restricted Feeding: The fascinating mice study from 2012:**
  Hatori, M., Vollmers, C., Zarrinpar, A., DiTacchio, L., Bushong, E. A., Gill, S., Leblanc, M., Chaix, A., Joens, M., Fitzpatrick, J. A. J., Ellisman, M. H., & Panda, S. (2012). Time-Restricted Feeding without Reducing Caloric Intake Prevents Metabolic Diseases in Mice Fed a High-Fat Diet. *Cell Metabolism, 15*(6), 848–860. https://doi.org/10.1016/j.cmet.2012.04.019
- **Melatonin supplements: Impact of dose and timing:**
  Burgess, H. J., Revell, V. L., Molina, T. A., & Eastman, C. I. (2010). Human Phase Response Curves to Three Days of Daily Melatonin: 0.5 mg *Versus* 3.0 mg. *The Journal of Clinical Endocrinology & Metabolism, 95*(7), 3325–3331. https://doi.org/10.1210/jc.2009-2590
- **Which supplements help with sleep:**
  Chan, V., & Lo, K. (2022). Efficacy of dietary supplements on improving sleep quality: A systematic review and meta-analysis. *Postgraduate Medical Journal, 98*(1158), 285–293. https://doi.org/10.1136/postgradmedj-2020-139319

Day 6: Consistency

- **Currently the most popular book on sleep**:
  Walker, M. (2017). Why we sleep: Unlocking the power of sleep and dreams. Simon and Schuster.

- **A book on circadian health as a therapy for mood disorders:**
  Wirz-Justice, A., Benedetti, F. & Terman, M. Chronotherapeutics for Affective Disorders: A Clinician's Manual for Light and Wake Therapy, 2nd, revised edition. (Karger Medical and Scientific Publishers, 2013).

Day 7: Your future as an early riser

- **Currently the most popular book on habit-building:**
  Clear, J. (2018). *Atomic habits: tiny changes, remarkable results : an easy & proven way to build good habits & break bad ones.* New York, New York, Avery, an imprint of Penguin Random House.

Extra: Cheat Days

- **Light timing influences circadian rhythm more than sleep timing:**
  Duffy, J. F., Kronauer, R. E. & Czeisler, C. A. Phase-shifting human circadian rhythms: influence of sleep timing, social contact and light exposure. J Physiol 495 (Pt 1), 289–297 (1996).

References

1. Facer-Childs, E. R., Middleton, B., Skene, D. J. & Bagshaw, A. P. Resetting the late timing of 'night owls' has a positive impact on mental health and performance. *Sleep Medicine* **60**, 236–247 (2019).
2. Brown, T. M. *et al.* Recommendations for daytime, evening, and nighttime indoor light exposure to best support physiology, sleep, and wakefulness in healthy adults. *PLOS Biology* **20**, e3001571 (2022).
3. Gardiner, C. *et al.* The effect of caffeine on subsequent sleep: A systematic review and meta-analysis. *Sleep Medicine Reviews* **69**, 101764 (2023).
4. Walker, M. *Why We Sleep: Unlocking the Power of Sleep and Dreams.* (Simon and Schuster, 2017).
5. Huberman, A. Master Your Sleep & Be More Alert When Awake - Huberman Lab.
6. Bowler, J. & Bourke, P. Facebook use and sleep quality: Light interacts with socially induced alertness. *British Journal of Psychology* **110**, 519–529 (2019).
7. Hern, A. Netflix's biggest competitor? Sleep. *The Guardian* (2017).
8. Kleitman, N. *Sleep and Wakefulness as Alternating Phases in the Cycle of Existence.* (Chicago, 1939).
9. Roenneberg, Pilz, Zerbini, & Winnebeck. Chronotype and Social Jetlag: A (Self-) Critical Review. *Biology* **8**, 54 (2019).
10. Roenneberg, T., Allebrandt, K. V., Merrow, M. & Vetter, C. Social jetlag and obesity. *Current Biology* **22**, 939–943 (2012).
11. Baron, K. G. & Reid, K. J. Circadian misalignment and health. *International Review of Psychiatry* **26**, 139–154 (2014).
12. Makarem, N., Paul, J., Giardina, E.-G. V., Liao, M. & Aggarwal, B. Evening Chronotype is Associated with Poor Cardiovascular Health and Adverse Health Behaviors in a Diverse Population of Women. *Chronobiology international* **37**, 673 (2020).
13. Ekiz Erim, S. & Sert, H. The relationship between chronotype and obesity: A systematic review. *Chronobiol Int* **40**, 529–541 (2023).
14. Merikanto, I. *et al.* Associations of Chronotype and Sleep With Cardiovascular Diseases and Type 2 Diabetes. *http://dx.doi.org/10.3109/07420528.2012.741171* **30**, 470–477 (2013).

15. Merikanto, I. & Partonen, T. Eveningness increases risks for depressive and anxiety symptoms and hospital treatments mediated by insufficient sleep in a population-based study of 18,039 adults. *Depression and Anxiety* **38**, 1066–1077 (2021).
16. Ward, E. M. *et al.* Carcinogenicity of night shift work. *The Lancet Oncology* **20**, 1058–1059 (2019).
17. Khalsa, S. B. S., Jewett, M. E., Cajochen, C. & Czeisler, C. A. A phase response curve to single bright light pulses in human subjects. *Journal of Physiology* **549**, 945–952 (2003).
18. Wright, K. P. *et al.* Entrainment of the Human Circadian Clock to the Natural Light-Dark Cycle. *Current Biology* **23**, 1554–1558 (2013).
19. Stothard, E. R. *et al.* Circadian Entrainment to the Natural Light-Dark Cycle Across Seasons and the Weekend. *Curr Biol* **27**, 508–513 (2017).
20. Chang, A.-M. *et al.* Human responses to bright light of different durations. *The Journal of Physiology* **590**, 3103–3112 (2012).
21. Giménez, M. C. *et al.* Effects of artificial dawn on subjective ratings of sleep inertia and dim light melatonin onset. *Chronobiology International* **27**, 1219–1241 (2010).
22. Gabel, V. *et al.* Effects of Artificial Dawn and Morning Blue Light on Daytime Cognitive Performance, Well-being, Cortisol and Melatonin Levels. *Chronobiology International* **30**, 988–997 (2013).
23. Czeisler, C. A. *et al.* Stability, precision, and near-24-hour period of the human circadian pacemaker. *Science* **284**, 2177–2181 (1999).
24. Chang, A.-M., Scheer, F. A. J. L. & Czeisler, C. A. The human circadian system adapts to prior photic history. *The Journal of Physiology* **589**, 1095–1102 (2011).
25. Golden, R. N. *et al.* The Efficacy of Light Therapy in the Treatment of Mood Disorders: A Review and Meta-Analysis of the Evidence. *https://doi.org/10.1176/appi.ajp.162.4.656* **162**, 656–662 (2005).
26. Pavlov, I. P. *Pavlov on the Conditional Reflex: Papers, 1903-1936.* (Oxford University Press, 2023).
27. Uyama, S. How To Love Waking Up: A Hands-On Guide To Becoming A M.... https://www.goodreads.com/book/show/30121979-how-to-love-waking-up.
28. Eyal, N. *Hooked: How to Build Habit-Forming Products.* (Penguin, 2014).
29. Scullin, M. K., Krueger, M. L., Ballard, H. K., Pruett, N. & Bliwise, D. L. The Effects of Bedtime Writing on Difficulty Falling Asleep: A Polysomnographic Study Comparing To-Do Lists and Completed Activity Lists. *J Exp Psychol Gen* **147**, 139–146 (2018).
30. Kräuchi, K., Cajochen, C. & Wirz-Justice, A. Waking up properly: Is there a role of thermoregulation in sleep inertia? *Journal of Sleep Research* **13**, 121–127 (2004).

31. Kräuchi, K., Cajochen, C., Werth, E. & Wirz-Justice, A. Functional link between distal vasodilation and sleep-onset latency? *American Journal of Physiology - Regulatory Integrative and Comparative Physiology* **278**, (2000).
32. Lok, R. *et al.* Bright Light Decreases Peripheral Skin Temperature in Healthy Men: A Forced Desynchrony Study Under Dim and Bright Light (II). *J Biol Rhythms* **37**, 417–428 (2022).
33. McHill, A. W., Smith, B. J. & Wright, K. P. Effects of caffeine on skin and core temperatures, alertness, and recovery sleep during circadian misalignment. *J Biol Rhythms* **29**, 131–143 (2014).
34. Kvam, S., Kleppe, C. L., Nordhus, I. H. & Hovland, A. Exercise as a treatment for depression: A meta-analysis. *Journal of Affective Disorders* **202**, 67–86 (2016).
35. Elwood, P. *et al.* Healthy Lifestyles Reduce the Incidence of Chronic Diseases and Dementia: Evidence from the Caerphilly Cohort Study. *PLOS ONE* **8**, e81877 (2013).
36. Kovac, K. *et al.* The impact of a short burst of exercise on sleep inertia. *Physiol Behav* **242**, 113617 (2021).
37. Youngstedt, S. D., Elliott, J. A. & Kripke, D. F. Human circadian phase–response curves for exercise. *The Journal of Physiology* **597**, 2253–2268 (2019).
38. Buijze, G. A., Sierevelt, I. N., van der Heijden, B. C. J. M., Dijkgraaf, M. G. & Frings-Dresen, M. H. W. The Effect of Cold Showering on Health and Work: A Randomized Controlled Trial. *PLoS One* **11**, e0161749 (2016).
39. 6 cold shower benefits to consider. https://www.uclahealth.org/news/6-cold-shower-benefits-consider.
40. The Best Temperature for Sleep. *Cleveland Clinic* https://health.clevelandclinic.org/what-is-the-ideal-sleeping-temperature-for-my-bedroom/ (2021).
41. Matthew Walker: Why Is It Essential To Make Time For Sleep? *NPR* https://www.npr.org/2021/02/05/964209001/matthew-walker-why-is-it-essential-to-make-time-for-sleep (2021).
42. Dahl, M. Sleep Hack: Keep Your Feet Outside Your Covers. *The Cut* https://www.thecut.com/2014/08/sleep-hack-keep-one-foot-outside-your-covers.html (2014).
43. Haghayegh, S., Khoshnevis, S., Smolensky, M. H., Diller, K. R. & Castriotta, R. J. Before-bedtime passive body heating by warm shower or bath to improve sleep: A systematic review and meta-analysis. *Sleep Medicine Reviews* **46**, 124–135 (2019).
44. Ko, Y. & Lee, J.-Y. Effects of feet warming using bed socks on sleep quality and thermoregulatory responses in a cool environment. *J Physiol Anthropol* **37**, 13 (2018).

45. Mistlberger, R. E. Food as circadian time cue for appetitive behavior. *F1000Res* **9**, F1000 Faculty Rev-61 (2020).
46. Wehrens, S. M. T. *et al.* Meal Timing Regulates the Human Circadian System. *Curr Biol* **27**, 1768-1775.e3 (2017).
47. Gu, C. *et al.* Metabolic Effects of Late Dinner in Healthy Volunteers—A Randomized Crossover Clinical Trial. *The Journal of Clinical Endocrinology & Metabolism* **105**, 2789–2802 (2020).
48. Duan, D., Gu, C., Polotsky, V. Y., Jun, J. C. & Pham, L. V. Effects of Dinner Timing on Sleep Stage Distribution and EEG Power Spectrum in Healthy Volunteers. *Nat Sci Sleep* **13**, 601–612 (2021).
49. Pot, G. K., Almoosawi, S. & Stephen, A. M. Meal irregularity and cardiometabolic consequences: results from observational and intervention studies. *Proceedings of the Nutrition Society* **75**, 475–486 (2016).
50. Huberman, A. Dr. Satchin Panda: Intermittent Fasting to Improve Health, Cognition & Longevity - Huberman Lab.
51. Gabel, K. & Varady, K. A. Current research: effect of time restricted eating on weight and cardiometabolic health. *The Journal of Physiology* **600**, 1313–1326 (2022).
52. Mitchell, S. J. *et al.* Daily Fasting Improves Health and Survival in Male Mice Independent of Diet Composition and Calories. *Cell Metab* **29**, 221-228.e3 (2019).
53. Hatori, M. *et al.* Time-Restricted Feeding without Reducing Caloric Intake Prevents Metabolic Diseases in Mice Fed a High-Fat Diet. *Cell Metabolism* **15**, 848–860 (2012).
54. Ashtary-Larky, D. *et al.* Effects of intermittent fasting combined with resistance training on body composition: a systematic review and meta-analysis. *Physiol Behav* **237**, 113453 (2021).
55. Liu, J., Yi, P. & Liu, F. The Effect of Early Time-Restricted Eating vs Later Time-Restricted Eating on Weight Loss and Metabolic Health. *J Clin Endocrinol Metab* **108**, 1824–1834 (2023).
56. Goodhines, P. A., Gellis, L. A., Ansell, E. B. & Park, A. Cannabis and alcohol use for sleep aid: A daily diary investigation. *Health Psychology* **38**, 1036–1047 (2019).
57. Ebrahim, I. O., Shapiro, C. M., Williams, A. J. & Fenwick, P. B. Alcohol and Sleep I: Effects on Normal Sleep. *Alcoholism: Clinical and Experimental Research* **37**, 539` – 549 (2013).
58. Pietilä, J. *et al.* Acute Effect of Alcohol Intake on Cardiovascular Autonomic Regulation During the First Hours of Sleep in a Large Real-World Sample of Finnish Employees: Observational Study. *JMIR Ment Health* **5**, e23 (2018).

59. Burgess, H. J., Revell, V. L., Molina, T. A. & Eastman, C. I. Human Phase Response Curves to Three Days of Daily Melatonin: 0.5 mg *Versus* 3.0 mg. *The Journal of Clinical Endocrinology & Metabolism* **95**, 3325–3331 (2010).
60. Cheng, D. C. Y. *et al.* The efficacy of combined bright light and melatonin therapies on sleep and circadian outcomes: A systematic review. *Sleep Med Rev* **58**, 101491 (2021).
61. Auger, R. R. *et al.* Clinical Practice Guideline for the Treatment of Intrinsic Circadian Rhythm Sleep-Wake Disorders: Advanced Sleep-Wake Phase Disorder (ASWPD), Delayed Sleep-Wake Phase Disorder (DSWPD), Non-24-Hour Sleep-Wake Rhythm Disorder (N24SWD), and Irregular Sleep-Wake Rhythm Disorder (ISWRD). An Update for 2015. *Journal of Clinical Sleep Medicine* **11**, 1199–1236.
62. Andersen, L. P. H., Gögenur, I., Rosenberg, J. & Reiter, R. J. The Safety of Melatonin in Humans. *Clin Drug Investig* **36**, 169–175 (2016).
63. Erland, L. A. E. & Saxena, P. K. Melatonin Natural Health Products and Supplements: Presence of Serotonin and Significant Variability of Melatonin Content. *J Clin Sleep Med* **13**, 275–281 (2017).
64. Chan, V. & Lo, K. Efficacy of dietary supplements on improving sleep quality: a systematic review and meta-analysis. *Postgraduate Medical Journal* **98**, 285–293 (2022).
65. Gotzler, M. Über Vollmondfeste, Kunstlicht und gesunde Solarien – Flowgrade Show Episode 42 mit Alexander Wunsch - Flowgrade.
66. Kudrnáčová, M. & Kudrnáč, A. Better sleep, better life? testing the role of sleep on quality of life. *PLOS ONE* **18**, e0282085 (2023).
67. Genzel, L. *et al.* Sleep timing is more important than sleep length or quality for medical school performance. *Chronobiol Int* **30**, 766–771 (2013).
68. LeGates, T. A. *et al.* Aberrant light directly impairs mood and learning through melanopsin-expressing neurons. *Nature 2012 491:7425* **491**, 594–598 (2012).
69. Davidson, A. J. *et al.* Chronic jet-lag increases mortality in aged mice. *Curr Biol* **16**, R914-916 (2006).
70. Torquati, L., Mielke, G. I., Brown, W. J., Burton, N. W. & Kolbe-Alexander, T. L. Shift Work and Poor Mental Health: A Meta-Analysis of Longitudinal Studies. *Am J Public Health* **109**, e13–e20 (2019).
71. Short, M. A. & Louca, M. Sleep deprivation leads to mood deficits in healthy adolescents. *Sleep Med* **16**, 987–993 (2015).
72. Oldham, M. A. & Ciraulo, D. A. Bright light therapy for depression: a review of its effects on chronobiology and the autonomic nervous system. *Chronobiol Int* **31**, 305–319 (2014).

73. Geoffroy, P. A., Schroder, C. M., Reynaud, E. & Bourgin, P. Efficacy of light therapy versus antidepressant drugs, and of the combination versus monotherapy, in major depressive episodes: A systematic review and meta-analysis. *Sleep Med Rev* **48**, 101213 (2019).
74. Wirz-Justice, A. *et al.* A randomized, double-blind, placebo-controlled study of light therapy for antepartum depression. *J Clin Psychiatry* **72**, 986–993 (2011).
75. Hill, V. M., Rebar, A. L., Ferguson, S. A., Shriane, A. E. & Vincent, G. E. Go to bed! A systematic review and meta-analysis of bedtime procrastination correlates and sleep outcomes. *Sleep Medicine Reviews* **66**, 101697 (2022).
76. Hublin, C. & Kaprio, J. Chronotype and mortality - a 37-year follow-up study in Finnish adults. *Chronobiol Int* **40**, 841–849 (2023).
77. Lally, P., van Jaarsveld, C. H. M., Potts, H. W. W. & Wardle, J. How are habits formed: Modelling habit formation in the real world. *European Journal of Social Psychology* **40**, 998–1009 (2010).
78. Clear, J. How Long Does it Actually Take to Form a New Habit? (Backed by Science). *James Clear* https://jamesclear.com/new-habit (2014).
79. Duffy, J. F., Kronauer, R. E. & Czeisler, C. A. Phase-shifting human circadian rhythms: influence of sleep timing, social contact and light exposure. *J Physiol* **495 (Pt 1)**, 289–297 (1996).
80. Sandhu, A., Seth, M. & Gurm, H. S. Daylight savings time and myocardial infarction. *Open Heart* **1**, e000019 (2014).
81. Tyler, J. *et al.* Genomic heterogeneity affects the response to Daylight Saving Time. *Sci Rep* **11**, 14792 (2021).

About us: Team Zeitgeber

We are Saeed, Klara, Simon & Marian (f.l.t.r.) and have set out to empower people by giving them the tools to shape their own morning experience and start their day the way they want to. Driven by the desire to help ourselves getting up in the morning, we started to look for solutions, tested gadgets, talked to scientists and eventually ended up building our own dawn simulation system to implement all our findings. This is how our startup "Zeitgeber" came to be. For more information visit www.zeitgeber.at.

Our vision is to make circadian health mainstream and normal.

We are proud to be scientifically advised by some of the world's leading researchers in the field of chronotherapy and circadian rhythm, Dr. Michael Terman and Prof. Jamie Zeitzer. Team Zeitgeber is a partner of the "CET - Center for Environmental Therapeutics", a US-based non-profit organization supporting light therapy and circadian health.

Our dedication to research has led to the knowledge presented in this book, if you want to know more about how and why our biological rhythms govern our daily lives, we can greatly encourage you to read through some of the references we listed in the back of this book. We would also love to hear from you and your personal experiences directly. Please don't hesitate to reach out to us on Reddit (*r/lovemornings*) or via email: hello@love-mornings.com.

Thank you for your trust and have a great morning!

Here are your
course materials!

MY MORNING ROUTINE

TIME	ACTIVITY

MY EVENING ROUTINE

TIME	ACTIVITY

Love Mornings - Checklist *Example*

Fill out daily. Each column represents one night of the course. Start with the first evening and continue filling out on the next morning.

Evenings

	Night 1	2	3	4	5	6	7
Only dim light after... 9 pm	✓	✓	☐	☐	✓	✓	☐
No caffeine after noon	✓	✓	✓	✓	✓	✓	✓
No smartphone after 9 pm	☐	✓	✓	☐	☐	✓	☐
Morning preparation	✓	✓	✓	☐	✓	✓	✓
Evening routine			✓	☐	✓	✓	✓
No exercise after 8 pm				✓	✓	✓	✓
No food after 7.30 pm					☐	✓	✓

Mornings

	Next morning 2	3	4	5	6	7
Bright light exposure	✓	✓	✓	✓	✓	✓
Morning routine		✓	✓	✓	✓	✓
Short burst of exercise			☐	✓	✓	✓
Cold shower			✓	✓	✓	✓

Love Mornings - Checklist *Example*

Target Bedtime: *10.30 pm*   Target Wake time: *06.45 am*

My personal why

I want to get up early to have time to study in order to ace my exam next month.

Signature *Ulfa*

	Night 1	2	3	4	5	6	7
Bedtime	10.45	10.35	10.20	11.30	10.35	10.30	10.30
Wake-up time	6.45	6.55	6.45	7.30	6.45	6.45	6.45

How refreshed did you feel when you woke up? (very refreshed ↑ not at all refreshed)

	1	2	3	4	5	6	7
very refreshed	○	○	○	○	○	⊗	⊗
	⊗	○	○	○	⊗	○	○
	○	○	⊗	○	○	○	○
	○	⊗	○	○	○	○	○
not at all refreshed	○	○	○	⊗	○	○	○

How much did you love your morning? (loved very much ↑ did not love at all)

	1	2	3	4	5	6	7
loved very much	○	○	○	○	⊗	⊗	⊗
	○	⊗	⊗	○	○	○	○
	⊗	○	○	○	○	○	○
	○	○	○	⊗	○	○	○
did not love at all	○	○	○	○	○	○	○

Love Mornings - Checklist

Fill out daily. Each column represents one night of the course. Start with the first evening and continue filling out on the next morning.

Evenings

Night	1	2	3	4	5	6	7
Only dim light after...	☐	☐	☐	☐	☐	☐	☐
	☐	☐	☐	☐	☐	☐	☐
	☐	☐	☐	☐	☐	☐	☐
	☐	☐	☐	☐	☐	☐	☐
Evening routine			☐	☐	☐	☐	☐
				☐	☐	☐	☐
					☐	☐	☐

Mornings

Next morning	2	3	4	5	6	7
	☐	☐	☐	☐	☐	☐
Morning routine		☐	☐	☐	☐	☐
			☐	☐	☐	☐
			☐	☐	☐	☐

Find a bigger version to print out here:

Love Mornings - Checklist

Target Bedtime: Target Wake time:

My personal why

....

....

Signature

____

	Night 1	2	3	4	5	6	7
Bedtime							
Wake-up time							

How refreshed did you feel when you woke up?

very refreshed ↑ not at all refreshed

1	2	3	4	5	6	7
○○○○○	○○○○○	○○○○○	○○○○○	○○○○○	○○○○○	○○○○○

How much did you love your morning?

loved very much ↑ did not love at all

1	2	3	4	5	6	7
○○○○○	○○○○○	○○○○○	○○○○○	○○○○○	○○○○○	○○○○○

Printed in Poland
by Amazon Fulfillment
Poland Sp. z o.o., Wrocław

29746949R00063